W9-BSC-074

BUILT TO
SUCK

IDEAPRESS
PUBLISHING

BUILT TO
SUCK

The Inevitable Demise
of the Corporation
... and How to Save It?

JOSEPH JAFFE

AUTHOR OF *FLIP THE FUNNEL*

IDEAPRESS
PUBLISHING

Proudly printed in the United States by Ideapress Publishing.

IDEAPRESS PUBLISHING | WWW.IDEAPRESSPUBLISHING.COM

All trademarks are the property of their respective companies.

COVER DESIGN BY DESIGNCROWD

Cataloging-in-Publication Data is on file with the Library of Congress.

ISBN: 978-1-940858-88-3

SPECIAL SALES

Ideapress Books are available at a special discount for bulk purchases for sales promotions and premiums, educational institutions or for use in corporate training programs. Special editions, including personalized covers, custom forewords and bonus content are also available. For more information, email info@ideapresspublishing.com

As always, I want to dedicate this book to my core.

To my wife, Terri. You deserve a medal of valor for putting up (and continuing to put up) with me. Our relationship was tested when you copyedited this manuscript, and I had to deal with your "constructive criticism." Happy to admit that you were right on pretty much all counts!

To my daughter, Amber—my best intern who decided to follow a college business path. Don't emulate me; leave me in your dust!

To my son, Aaron. If professional soccer and Fortnite battles don't work out, there's always that incredible brain you have on your shoulders.

To my son, Jack. Your talent and potential are overpowering. Believe in yourself, take a chance on yourself, and go for it. Anything is possible.

To my dog, Sammy (yes, I went there.) Your unconditional love for me is unsurpassed, except for....

My mother. The original survival planner. You are a cancer survivor, but you've been surviving (and thriving) since I can remember.

I love you all.

And finally...to Mike Hoff, the legend.

TABLE OF CONTENTS

SECTION 4: PRAGMATISM

SECTION 5: HANGOVER

A NOTE ABOUT THE COVER

This book is all about eating the dog food. You'll see exactly what I mean when you read my Uber story toward the end of the book.

This book is about recognizing a new world and a new world order. It's one in which corporations are not welcome, and are few and far between.

This is why I went with Ideapress as my publisher. It was started by a peer, fellow thought leader, and author who recognized that the traditional world of publishing was archaic, outdated, and, quite frankly, irrelevant.

It's also why I utilized currnt,[1] the Fresh Knowledge Network, to help research and validate my thesis. The thread can be found at https://currnt.com/s507/the-demise-of-the-corporation.

It's why I turned to DesignCrowd to utilize the wisdom of the crowds to create my cover. Thomas B. from Denmark...you rock.

I wrote the brief and hoped for a scene right out of *The Walking Dead*.

I got what I wanted; the dust has settled. The sky is blue. It is a new day. There is a new hope, but not before The Corporapocylpse has settled in. The world of the corporation has waned. The graveyard of what was once the mighty and infallible is now littered with death, decay, and the terminally ill.

Hope? Sure, there's hope. That's why some of the neon logos of companies that may seem familiar to you are not completely extinguished. Yet. Dramatic? Overdramatic? Melodramatic? Perhaps; perhaps not. Read on, and judge for yourself. Ultimately, how you interpret and internalize the information will determine on which side of history you will fall.

LEAVING A LEGACY

W HAT MOTIVATES YOU? WHAT GETS YOU OUT OF BED IN THE morning? What keeps you up at night? What defines you? When all is said and done, what will you be known for when you're done? What will you leave behind? When you're elected to the Hall of Fame, what will be your *coup de grâce*?

For some people, it's money. Fortune. And why not? Those of us who live in a capitalistic world and society are measured—or measured up—with key performance indicators such as net worth, wealth, status, and the like.

For others, it's fame. We live in an age of celebrity. One year, I returned from South by Southwest (SxSW), the annual interactive, music, and film festival in Austin, and was asked about my highlights. Rather than talk about artificial intelligence, robotics, or the next big mobile app, I listed meeting Grumpy Cat, running into (literally) Guillermo from *The Jimmy Kimmel Show*, and seeing Will Ferrell!

Figure 0.1 - Running into Guillermo at SxSW (literally)

In the world of reality television, relative unknowns can go from zero to hero in the blink of a made-for-TV meltdown—and the bigger the meltdown, the more their friends, fans, and followers will skyrocket.

Social media has become both a lubricant and an accelerant to *weblebrity* status. Today, one is able to project one's (Inter)net worth through verification on Facebook and Twitter, or as a LinkedIn "In"fluencer.

Everyone wants to be a star, and now it's your turn—depending on the type of person you are. To that end, I suspect there will be two groups of people who read this book: the rock stars who stand with me (*you're not telling us anything we don't already know*) and the disa-stars who reject me (*we don't believe him. Things aren't that bad.*)[1]

Many terrific books have been written on the themes I'll touch upon in this book: from Clayton Christensen's *The Innovator's Dilemma* to Eric Ries' *Lean Startup* to Simon Sinek's *Start with Why* to the granddaddy of them all, *Good to Great* and *Built to Last* by Jim Collins.

Homage to Jim Collins (We Are Not Worthy)

Jim Collins is, in many respects, the opposite of me. He is professional, mature, respectful, smart, disciplined, good-looking...I could go on. In 1997, he wrote *Built to Last,* in which he introduced his research and thinking around what he called "visionary companies," and debunked 12 myths associated with them.

Later in the book, I will revisit and reconcile the seemingly contradictory perspectives between *Built to Suck* and *Built to Last.*

Each of these books holds keys to corporate success in its own right, and yet large companies remain terminally ill and on life support. With 52 percent of the Fortune 500 from 2002 no longer on this esteemed list, I think it's clear we need to connect the dots between these various tomes and escalate the urgency associated with figuring out what's going on around most large organizations nowadays. I'd like to believe calling the corporation an endangered species accomplishes just that. I'll explain why I believe this, and offer a sizeable chunk of both empirical and anecdotal evidence to back up my thesis.

I'll also pepper in a bunch of case studies—some you're familiar with, and some that are completely off the beaten track. In the case of the former, I'll bring a unique perspective to the table that paints a different picture. When I refer to the usual suspects such as Amazon, Netflix, Nike, or Starbucks, I want you to see that the very reason they are successful is because they have adopted many of the principles mentioned in *Built to Suck.*

This book is an opinion piece. A rather large op-ed. I don't expect you to agree with everything I say. I am calling it like I see it — in this case by declaring a corporate state of emergency.

Being inspired is just not good enough anymore. What is required is action. My goal is to get you to take action. I want you to feel something. Pleasure is fine, but pain is even better.

Later in the book, I'll introduce you to the Survival Planning Canvas. This is a proprietary planning tool and process I created to help you hone and intensify your survival instinct. You'll need it to function at full capacity as you develop your survival plan, and, ultimately, your growth plan. At the end of the day, it's all about growth: discovering it if you're a startup, or returning to it if you're a legacy corporation. For now, remember this: until you have ensured your immediate survival, you'll never be able to achieve *thrival*.

Warning: what follows is fast-paced and intense. Get used to it, as this is just a small taste of normal life; business as usual in today's operating environment. If you suffer from anxiety and/or are on medication, please proceed with caution, and at your own risk.

"It is not the smartest of species that survives, nor the most intelligent; but rather the one that is the most adaptable to change."
—Charles Darwin

SECTION 1:

PURGATORY

CHAPTER 1

LIFE SUCKS

THE WORLD IS IN CHAOS. WE'RE MELTING, BOILING, FLOODING, UNDER SIEGE by bots, trolls, fake news, and alternative facts, and moving further and further apart toward the extremes of left and right. On any given day, we're on the verge of World War III (or perhaps it will already have happened by the time this is published.)

Natural-born leaders are in short supply. In fact, it seems like the joke is on us, as the unwitting cast of a global reality TV show.

With so much tumult going on in the world, we've retreated far into our own shells. When we emerge from hiding, it appears we've gone back in time to 1940, when nationalism and isolationism were just for the cool kids.

Culture and religion are under threat, hostage to a death match of conservative and liberal extremes. Even public restrooms aren't safe anymore from partisan outrage and contempt.

The Barnum and Bailey Circus may have (been forced to) closed down in the United States in 2017, but it has seemingly been resurrected in the Capitol building. With Congress approval ratings so low, the only thing left to do is put a blue or red clown nose on the officials we help to elect in the first place.

I NEED A HERO

Sing it, Bonnie Tyler, sing it!

Surely, there is someone or something out there to help save the day?

Of course there is. His name is Watson. He's super intelligent. He's getting smarter by the day, and will soon be able to tell us hour-by-hour weather predictions with 60 percent probability (according to the European model) or 70 percent probability (according to the international model). He's going to cure cancer. No, he isn't.

Hailed as the "medical messiah" in 2013, Watson received billions of dollars to end cancer. In 2018, the health and medical website stat.com reported that *"IBM's Watson supercomputer recommended 'unsafe and incorrect' cancer treatments, internal documents show."* Watson Health has since begun laying off an undisclosed number of employees.

With Watson exposed as the false Messiah, enter social media to save the day—the original invitation to "join the conversation." (I think someone wrote a book on that.) It's God's gift to customer service in just 140 to 280 characters—the promise of perfect information and complete transparency as a way to eradicate corruption, evil, bullying, monopolies, and identity thieves.

So, how's that working out for ya?

Figure 1.1 - Strange Bedfellows

The truth is, we've never been or felt so alone. Turns out this global village isn't a small world, after all, but rather a microcosm for the rich getting richer, the lonely getting lonelier, and the lazy getting lazier.

We're depressed. We're overmedicated. It's depressing unless you work for a pharmaceutical company cashing in on all this misery.

Raise your hand if you've forgotten what your child's voice sounds like. Family interaction has been replaced by group texts; acts of kindness involve "liking recent posts;" and threats about "cutting you off" no longer apply to inheritance, but to the trough of data and screen time.

Well, at least there's the purity of Hollywood and the thrill of losing ourselves in the escapism of fiction and fantasy. So, did you hear the one about the movie mogul who fondled one intern too many? Prepare to be transported away to yet another Marvel sequel as you munch on overpriced, sodium-infused popcorn and recline in your lie-flat seats.

Enter the "real-life" heroes to save the day: corporations and their laboratory-grown brands! Life will always be beautiful when we have Tide to Go. Gillette is, after all, "the best a man can get." Just ask Roger Federer. VW is the car of the nation(alist). And the sugary bubbly goodness of a Coca-Cola, with new packaging designed to make it look similar to Diet Coke or Coke Zero, is sure to bait and switch a whole swath of aspiring diabetics.

Figure 1.2 - Spot the Difference

Hooray, consumerism. Hooray, commerce. Hooray, medical marijuana. Hooray, branding. Hooray, media. Hooray, advertising.

Not so fast. More than half of Fortune 500 companies and their precious brands in 2017-2018 experienced declining revenues, despite a continued **increase** in media spending.[1] Maybe we can't advertise our way out of this mess. Perhaps we'll need to get used to "getting less from more," as prices of a Super Bowl spot continue to rise year after year. It makes complete sense in an upside-down world.

Fear not...we have the darling startups to save the day. Just ask Alexa to ask Uber's CEO, Travis Kalanick, and he'll tell you firsthand. Hang on, I apparently just got an out-of-office auto-response saying he's taken a leave of absence, and should be back when we find out the results of Branson vs. Musk: Battle to the Moon (also known as Fast 'n' Furious '26).

This is just the tip of the iceberg.

If the optimist says the glass is half full and the pessimist says it's half empty, the realist says the water is probably infected with lead poisoning. Just ask the poor residents of Flint, Michigan.

DON'T SHOOT THE MESSENGER

The time to ignore, overlook, diminish, forget, or deny is over. Business as we know it is anything but usual, and it is becoming quite clear that a line has been drawn: the line between the haves and have-nots.

So, if you're a shareholder looking to maximize your growth (or protect your assets), or a practitioner looking to hold onto your job, tenure, bonus, or cash-out, you're up shit creek without the proverbial paddle.

Figure 1.3 - Not My Problem

The truth hurts, but this isn't meant to be an exercise in futility or masochism. There's always hope. There's always a way forward. There *is* a scenario in which you could find yourself on the right side of history...as opposed to history itself...

CHAPTER 2

CHANGE SUCKS

A T THE CENTER OF THE HURRICANE THAT IS OUR LIVES IS THE "eye" of change, and if you think about it, there's a certain peace in coming to terms with the fact that the only guarantees in life are death, taxes...and change. Okay, and presidential tweets at 3 a.m. on a Sunday.

I have been writing about change for 15 years, and I don't think anything I've said over this period has been overhyped, exaggerated, or inaccurate—which is exactly why I'm telling you now that you ain't seen nothing yet!

WHERE DO I START?

You know this is all mainstreaming when you receive an e-mail from your father-in-law entitled "Wish I was 25" that pretty succinctly summarizes this perfect storm of change. And I didn't even need to forward it to ten friends in order to keep the chain going and avoid bad luck as a result!

You can read the full e-mail on www.builttosuck.com under the bonus content tab.

What really piqued my interest, though, was the "domino" effect of how this change will make its way through entire industries, and ultimately affect secondary or even tertiary industries.

Take 3-D printing, for example. A reduction of cost from $18,000 to $400 in just 10 years, coupled with speed improvements at 100X, have opened up countless new possibilities, including at-home printing of shoes, spare parts for airplanes, the space station, or even a six-story building in China. All of this has already happened!

In fact, by 2027, 10 percent of **everything** that's being produced will be 3D-printed.

Like the relationship between agriculture, aeroponics, and alternative food sources like insect protein. Or the connection between automotive and real estate: imagine parking lots being converted to parks thanks to self-driving cars. And what about insurance? Over a million lives will be saved every year due to a reduction in accidents. We're talking about a reduction from one accident every 60,000 miles (100,000 km) to one accident in 6 million miles (10 million km).

Or the intersection between pharmaceuticals, healthcare and insurance, with the introduction of the Tricorder X,[1] which will work with your phone to analyze 54 biomarkers and identify nearly any disease. It will be so cheap that in a few years, everyone on this planet will have nearly free access to world-class medical analysis.

All this sounds great, right? That is, unless you are directly (or even indirectly) affected by this change. Which, by the way, is pretty much all of us.

Take the legal profession, for example. There will be 90 percent fewer lawyers in the future, as people will be able to get legal advice within seconds at 90 percent accuracy. Clearly, some of this change is extremely good! Sorry, couldn't resist the obligatory lawyer joke. Now we just need to work on politicians, used-car salespeople, and advertising executives!

Perhaps these same fears are responsible for the waves of misguided nationalism, isolationism, and xenophobia spreading around the world? Perhaps this is less about letting outsiders into a country, and more about keeping them out of companies. In one word, jobs; in more words, inhibiting growth, progress, and the ability to earn an income.

This is where technology gets added into the change cocktail! Technology is the common thread in this unprecedented period of innovation, advancement, and transformation. It has destabilized the *status quo* and created a dystopian reality (as reflected in *Black Mirror*, or even as far back as *Blade Runner*) in which machines have already started to take over. Case in point: replacing tollbooth operators with epilepsy-inducing strobe-light cameras.

The destruction doesn't stop with humans. It applies equally to inanimate objects like bricks and mortar. We're seeing store closures happening with increasing frequency. While some people envision a retail Phoenix rising from the ashes, largely thanks to clichés like *phygical* (the nonsensical fusion between physical and digital), I would choose a different avian descriptor: the albatross around the neck of retail, which is causing massive aftershocks to be felt across ancillary industries such as real estate.

Think about it. How does a Westfield Mall survive when there are no longer anchor tenants? Empty malls will surely lead to a price correction in the commercial real-estate market. Decreased rental pricing may help in the short term, but it doesn't address the giant Amazon in the room, now, does it?

And it's not just retail being affected by these changes.

How do Hertz or Enterprise survive when there's Uber? Or Lyft? Or Via? Or Juno? Or Curb? Or Didi Chuxing (China)? Or Grab (Southeast Asia)? Or Ola (India)? Why would anyone need to rent a car anymore? And if so, what, exactly, are the benefits (or, in marketing speak, what is the differentiation) of doing so?

Give them credit for introducing perks like Satellite Radio, GPS, and an upgrade to the Corvette convertible; but even these have since been marginalized by the likes of a Sirius-XM app, Waze, and Sixt, respectively.

IF YOU CAN'T BEAT 'EM, BUY 'EM.

Credit where it's due: Avis purchased Zipcar in 2013 for $500 million. In 2017, they entered into an agreement with Uber to let drivers access vehicles through Zipcar, and in August 2018, they announced they would let drivers book Avis vehicles from the Lyft app. They also partnered with Waymo to manage a fleet of 600 self-driving cars.

Good for Avis, but what about automotive manufacturers? General Motors paid big money for product placement in the *Matrix* movie trilogy, while BMW did the same with *Mission Impossible*, but now they're shelling out top dollar for investments in the likes of Lyft ($500 million from GM) and Uber ($500 million from Toyota) or experimenting with the shared economy/ride-sharing business with models like ReachNow (BMW).

This is all happening before self-driving cars become the norm versus the exception. When that happens, the shit will surely hit the proverbial fan belt!

BACK TO THE FUTURE

In 2004, I wrote *Life After the 30-Second Spot* with the following stake in the ground: *"...in its existing form, the 30-second spot is either dead, dying, or has outlasted its usefulness."*

I predicted the future a full 10 years before October 21, 2015, the date immortalized in the DeLorean from *Back to the Future*. Interestingly enough, the DeLorean Motor Company (yes, it was real) filed for bankruptcy in 1982.

Figure 2.1 - Here Tomorrow. Gone Today.

Many predictions in this movie have come true, including personal drones and mobile payment technology. We saw smart clothing and wearable tech, waste-fueled cars, and more infamous inventions like hoverboards (ours burst into flames[2] when charged) and smart frames (remember Google Glass?)

And yes, even Donald Trump. Marty McFly's arch nemesis, Biff Tannen, was a wealthy casino owner who became president!

So, what about my predictions?

On the surface, it would appear that the 30-second spot is still blissfully unaware of the coming storm. Or at least it was until the end of 2016, when advertisers spent $72.09 billion on U.S. digital advertising, compared to TV spending, which accounted for $71.29 billion. Not exactly the beginning of the end, is it? Surely, this town is big enough for two cowboys?

Fast-forward to 2017, and the rot spreads to digital advertising, with bell-wether advertiser Procter & Gamble announcing that their business felt little negative impact after cutting $100 million in digital marketing spend in the second quarter.

This, coupled with the questionable accuracy of the metrics being used by juggernauts like Facebook , only served to taint the digital marketing arena even more.

And just when you thought 2019 would bring some relief, it appears that social media has become nothing more than a shill for snake oil, trolls, and pretty much any other nefarious, manipulative, and premeditated effort by illegitimate powers (let's include corporations in that mix!)

WAY BACK TO THE FUTURE

To debate the efficacy and longevity of the 30-second spot (which, I will point out, was always a metaphor for a traditional, linear, interruptive, irrelevant, one-size-fits-all, one-too-many, flawed business model) is a red herring. To really understand where the world is heading, it is worth going all the way back to...television. Specifically, *The Jetsons*.

The Jetsons debuted in 1962 on ABC, and predated *Back to the Future* with these accurate predications:

1. Robot servants (her name is Alexa)

2. Flat-screen TVs (big deal—they didn't exactly predict the curve, now, did they?)

3. Video chat (FaceTime)

4. Smart watches (Apple Watch)

5. Drones (sadly, check)

6. Robot maids (Roombas)

7. Digital newspaper (today's equivalent of the CD)

8. 3D-printed food

9. Pillcam

10. Space tourism (sorry, Elon and Richard, you weren't the first.)

There isn't really much left, if you think about it, except for teleportation and time travel, but enough about *Star Trek*.

Actually, hold that thought. Let's focus specifically on *Star Trek*.

STAR TREK: DESPERATION

In 2017, U.S. broadcast stalwart CBS boldly went where no network had gone before, unless you count Amazon Prime, Netflix, and HBO Go—in which case, there is nothing bold about this.

CBS announced the "launch" of the latest *Star Trek* franchise: *Discovery*, which debuted with a special two-part premiere on Sunday, September 24th at 8.30 p.m. EST. It followed NFL Football and *60 Minutes*. Episode 1, that is: the appetite-whetter for their new and debatably "improved" CBS All Access service. At $5.99 per month with advertising or a premium $9.99 per month without advertising, Episode 2 was just a sign-up away.

IDENTITY CRISIS

Why fault CBS for copying the industry gold standard, Netflix? Perhaps because this was just a cheap imitation. The pricing might be similar, but the service is anything but. For starters, Netflix is ad-free. CBS is stuck in the neutral zone, or, more accurately, purgatory. Their entire business model is about being ad-supported. By releasing premium programming for a subscription fee, they are essentially cannibalizing their own model. If the content is so great, why starve the rest of the non-paying public? And why is the paying public not being rewarded with the entire season released all at once, for an enticing and tasty "binge?" The only reward is more advertising!

This two-tiered structure, as it relates to advertising, runs the risk of confusion and customer dissatisfaction.

On the other end of the spectrum, let's assume for a moment that All Access becomes an overwhelming success. Now ABC, NBC, and Fox—and soon, a host of cable brands—follow suit. What happens to the already-overburdened cable bill? From the one-size-fits all monopolistic cable companies to the individual networks, all looking to get in on the mad scramble to the bottom of the barrel, when all of these à la carte subscriptions combine to become more expensive than before the cord was cut, it's a recipe for disaster.

Looks like both the cable companies and the networks are going to find themselves on the losing team, with Netflix, Amazon, and Hulu sitting pretty.

This could be a small step forward for CBS, only to take a giant leap backward. Why cannibalize your broader market by starving them of your best content? Trying to be an HBO or Netflix at this stage is not going to work. Not now. It involves too much of a dramatic shift, too late in the game. In any case, the evidence says they're not shifting dramatically at all, but shifting incrementally.

Instead, why not try and fix the advertising model in the digital world? And, until that happens, maximize ad revenue until its inevitable demise?

Sound like a bit of a contradiction? You're right. It is.

THE CATCH-22 OF CHANGE

A train is hurtling down the track at 300 mph, and the conductor gets word that a bridge the train will shortly cross is down. So, what does the conductor do, given that there are just minutes until impending doom? If he or she applies the brakes too gently, the train will almost certainly run out of time (and track) before it cascades over the bridge. On the flipside, if the conductor pulls the emergency brake, the train will almost certainly derail. Either way, lives will be lost.

So, what's the answer? There isn't one, as this isn't a riddle—it's life. However, if you want to look at this analogy as a solvable puzzle, apply some lateral thinking and find a happy ending like *"the conductor pulls out his Waze for Trains app, and uses the remote functionality to change tracks at a switching station that comes up just before the bridge."*

Figure 2.2 - The Catch-22 of Change

The image above is an original drawing I commissioned from the online freelance marketplace Fiverr—another example of an upstart startup destabilizing an incumbent industry and interrupting the status quo.

This moral of the story is all about the pace of change. Change too slowly, and you'll surely run out of runway or "tracks." Change too quickly, and you'll surely run out of cultural currency. Change is hard, and when people are not ready for it, too much change too soon can have a considerably adverse effect on morale, performance, and tenure.

Predictions are a dime a dozen. Some come to pass faster than we could ever have imagined. Some are woefully misguided. So, rather than betting the farm on one particular technology trend versus another, it is probably a wise move to work on developing your "change muscle:" in other words, your ability to successfully anticipate, adapt, and evolve at an increasingly regular rate.

CHAPTER 3

CORPORATIONS SUCK

'D LIKE TO TELL YOU THAT THE CORPORATE BUBBLE IS ABOUT TO burst, but I'd be lying. I'd be lying because it already has. May I submit the following evidence?

Exhibit A: As mentioned earlier, between 2016-2018, 50 percent of Fortune 500 companies had declining revenue in comparison with the prior year.

Exhibit B: 447 of the original Fortune 500 companies from 1955 (when the list was first created) are gone. 9 in 10. Let that sink in.

Exhibit C:

- 50 percent of Fortune 500 companies from 2000 have *disappeared*.
- 70 percent of Fortune 500 companies from 1990 have *disappeared*.

This is not fake news...unless you believe the CEO of Accenture, Pierre Nanterme, is a pathological liar!

Exhibit D: The future's so bleak, not even shades will help! Nearly 50 percent of the current S&P 500 will be replaced over the next ten years. In fact, according to Innosight, by 2027, the average tenure on the S&P 500 will be just 12 years.

.

If you're a stickler for methodology, the words *gone, disappeared, and replaced* from the earlier exhibits refer to the Fortune/S&P 500 lists. They cover going bankrupt, merging with (or being acquired by) another firm, *or companies that still exist, but have fallen from the top 500*. Don't get too excited, because there's one more exhibit....

Exhibit E: In 1967, the average lifespan of a company on the Fortune 500 was around 75 years. In 2018, it is less than 15 years. This does not mean "fell off the list;" it means "fell off the face of the earth." I wanted to make sure I sourced this correctly, and found a handful of corroborating data points from the likes of Credit Suisse and even General Stanley McChrystal in his book, *Team of Teams.*

Take a moment to introspect, ponder, wail, mourn, or whatever you need to do in order to recognize the start of the Corporate Purge. It's not a coincidence that we're seeing seismic changes in the birth, rise, and demise of the corporation as we knew it.

Do you care? Well, you should, if you work for one of these companies; if you have your 401K invested in said companies; if you are a shareholder in one of those companies; or if you are connected or interconnected in a supply chain or ecosystem in which one of these companies operates.

You should feel sick to your stomach. Or perhaps you just don't care anymore. Maybe you're in denial. Perhaps you just don't think it will happen to you.

I once asked a senior marketer why he made the poor decisions he did. Was it not obvious to him that the fruits of his labor had amounted to nothing more than a lemon? He responded candidly that the sycophants around him— well, he used the words "direct reports," and, in particular, his "agency"—had consistently told him how great he was, what a great job he was doing, and how much they loved the work. I appreciated his honestly about the ubiquitous and gratuitous enablement.

If you tell yourself a lie enough times and for long enough, you'll eventually start believing it... but ignoring reality is not advisable. No one wants to be the naked emperor.

THE ENTIRE BUSINESS MODEL OF BUSINESS IS FLAWED

My contention, and a central part of the hypothesis of this book, is that corporations are terminal. They are diseased, and stand little to no chance of survival.

The central operating system that powers the corporation, and will ultimately be its downfall, is SIZE. Scale, economies of scale, and the cost efficiencies of mass production served as catalysts for the original growth engine, but are now backfiring. Size is no longer a growth enabler; it's a growth inhibitor.

It has caused corporations to lose their edge—specifically their competitive edge. They are no longer equipped to adapt. To evolve. To change. They are simply too big and bureaucratic; too risk-averse and political.

They proudly crow about their 100+ years of history; their founder(s) who are almost always white males; their mission statement, which invariably mentions the word "market leader" or "leadership." They fail to recognize that their days are most certainly numbered. They are rudderless, and lost at sea.

Their inability to morph or pivot has put them on life support.

Think about this for a moment: *Uber, the world's largest taxi company, owns no vehicles. Facebook, the world's most popular media owner, creates no content. Alibaba, the most valuable retailer, has no inventory. And Airbnb, the world's largest accommodation provider, owns no real estate.*

What exactly do you do if you're a consumer packaged goods company? Or if you're a retailer? How can you compete when your entire stock in trade is tangible and durable in a physical world that is becoming ever more intangible, non-durable, and virtual? How do you compete if you are an 800-pound gorilla with legacy, incumbency, overhead, and cronyism baggage?

Amazon is a relative infant in corporate terms, having been founded in 1994. When do you think their only remaining competitor (at least in "books of scale") Barnes & Noble was founded? I'll reveal this shortly, but why not take a guess, and see if you are in the ballpark? No cheating!

In 2017, Amazon (we've since dropped the dot com), at 23 years young, undertook to open its second headquarters. To demonstrate how the balance of power has shifted, playful Jeff decided to make a game of this by opening this up to local, regional, and even state bidders to pitch for the privilege of hosting HQ2. By October, they had received 238 proposals from 54 states, provinces, districts, and territories in North America.

When was the last time you got municipalities to bid for your pollution-infested factories?

The winners were Crystal City, Virginia and Long Island City, in the Queens borough of New York, thanks largely to tax incentives and subsidies from the States. Governor Andrew Cuomo even offered to change his name to Amazon Cuomo if New York won the prize. Wonder if he'll follow through? On the flipside, New York State Assembly Member Ron Kim offered his alternative to gifting all this money to Amazon: wiping out student debt in his state!

We now return to our regularly-scheduled programming.

If you guessed Barnes & Noble was founded in 1984 (very Orwellian), you would have been off by only 100 years! Founded in 1886, Barnes & Noble will almost certainly not be around to celebrate their 150th anniversary in 2036. At a time when the bricks and mortar that make up the facade of their company are akin to cement shoes and a one-way trip to the bottom of the ocean, isn't it ironic that Amazon is opening up new headquarters? They are proudly purchasing brick-and-mortar retailers like Whole Foods, and taking on Weinsteinless Hollywood with original content like *The Man in the High Castle*, *Sneaky Pete*, and *The Marvelous Mrs. Maisel*.

The very size of companies and their desperate need for enormity and scale has become a vicious cycle, spiraling downward toward inevitable doom.

A POX ON YOUR BOARDROOM:
THE CURSE OF SHORT-TERMITIS

Eric Reynolds, Clorox's Chief Marketing Officer, gave a speech at a marketing conference in 2017 in which he spoke about a condition called *short-termitis*. There are about 554 responses on Google for this compound phrase, or 5.4 million if you expand it to include termite infestations, which I think is appropriate when considering the plague affecting so many companies these days.

Public companies suffer from *short-termitis*. It's a self-fulfilling, chronic, ultimately fatal disease that rots companies from the inside out. There is no known cure other than dulling the pain with acquisitions that purchase "revenue" rather than earning it through natural, organic, and deserved growth.

Specialists called consultants or private equity are called in to relieve the pain, but ultimately exacerbate or defer the inevitable death knell.

I'll say it again: The entire business model is flawed. It's mass-turbation of decadent proportions. Mass production. Mass media. Mass distribution.

No Mas(s)

In a classic chicken-and-egg scenario (apparently, it's the egg that came first), do we sell what we make, or do we make what we sell? In days of yore, it was the former. And by yore, I refer to the era of snake-oil salesmen—the glory days of *Mad Men*, when Don Draper lived the life of Riley, and life was good. Advertising created a self fulfilling prophecy in which gullible consumers lapped up beauties such as "blow in her face and she'll follow you anywhere, or "for a better start in life, start cola earlier" as a message to moms with young children.

Figure 3.1 - Our Embarrassing Past

To hit goals, from impressions to awareness to sales, it was good enough just to be good enough. Even though 50 percent of the population is dumber than the other half (your reaction to this statistic will instantly determine which half you belong to), being average was essentially above average. The one-size-fits-all approach, characterized by the spray-and-pray technique of mass communication, led to waste and irrelevant targeting (like exposing tampon advertising to males). This most certainly resulted in most people leaving the room to make a sandwich or take a whizz when the ads came on. Today, of course, there's built-in skip functionality in most set-top boxes and standalone DVRs, but now there's a much more sinister enemy among us: the impact of multiple screens.

It's not uncommon for my young son to adeptly multitask in front of three screens at once. Most of us struggle to pay attention with just one. And it's not a fair fight in the TV vs. phone death match. There is only one unanimous winner: the phone. Television has become background muzak, so if you think your 30-second spot has a snowball's chance of trumping yet another saga on Candy Crush, you are sorely mistaken.

According to a variety of research, the average attention span is down from 12 seconds in the year 2000 to eight seconds now.[1] That is less than the nine-second attention span of your average goldfish. I will stop short of attempting to deconstruct the proliferation of screens, the falling attention spans, and the drop in advertising efficacy. I will also not expand upon the differences between average and exceptional goldfish.

I will, however, strongly question the enduring longevity of advertising in **all** forms. Advertising is the poster child of the "sell what we make" era, and its lifespan is inextricably linked to that of the corporation. Not too long ago, it was a solid, reliable, dependable approach to base, build, and sustain a multi-billion-dollar business and brand. Today, it is an incredibly questionable and shaky methodology upon which to bet the farm (unless we're talking about the online game FarmVille.)

I believe it is borderline impossible to launch a business through advertising anymore. It didn't really work during the dot-com crash of 2000, and it hasn't really worked since. I can't recall a single case, and if you are smirking right now and can name one, go ahead and pat yourself on the back. While you're doing that, try and name four more. Should you pass that test, I will genuinely shake your 5-fingered hand while cautioning you that five cases are not exactly a ringing endorsement for an entire industry and practice, now, are they?

I will also remind you that not one of the startup giant success stories (Uber, Tesla, Xiaomi, WeWork, AirBnB, Amazon—the list goes on) used any form of mass/paid media advertising to launch and ride their initial hockey-stick growth curve.

Ironically, when Xiaomi (China's electronics giant, which was founded in 2010) chose to take out a full-page print ad in India in 2015—a market still grounded in a more traditional media infrastructure—it actually became a big deal and earned a lot of media attention!

Today, many of these companies have taken to advertising in order to _sustain_ their brands. This is considered a necessary evil as they themselves settle into the inevitable trappings of the early stages of suckage.

UNICORNS ASIDE, WHAT ABOUT THE REST OF THE ANIMALS?

...but advertising works, Joseph! When we spend money, sales go up (or don't go down) and when we don't, sales go down.

Correlation is not causation. There is so much waste built into this model, and yet somehow, we've come to recognize this as acceptable. That is, until revelations come out, like the aforementioned revelation from P&G about digital spend and sales.

THE UGLY TRUTH ABOUT ADVERTISING

Advertising may have one—make that two—uses left. It helps tell people things they might not have already known about things that might interest and/or benefit them. This is a dwindling _raison d'être_, thanks in large part to word of mouth and social media. Then there's the fact that it gainfully employs and supports many interconnected industries, and while I do like the idea of giving people jobs (shout out to my buddies at the Department of Homeland Security), giving someone a meaningless job is not reason enough to do it in the first place. Business is not charity. Again, just look at the myriad industries dropping employees like flies due to automation. So, why does advertising get a pass?

Most of the realities of advertising are ugly. Literally.

For a long time, advertising has been in the cosmetics business...as in putting lipstick on a pig. Most products are no different from their shelf-mates: conspicuously vanilla in terms of face value. Instead of demanding and delivering actual proof of product superiority, the only differentiation today comes in the form of brand communication. It's a fool's errand.

TAIL WAGGING THE DOG

So, do media and advertising sustain brands, or do brands sustain media and advertising? I don't think this is an unfair question to ask, and I don't know the answer, but it's probably enough to warrant an ethics investigation.

WHAT ARE WE DOING HERE, PEOPLE?

As the saying goes, *when digging oneself into a hole, the best thing to do is to stop digging*. At what point do we take a time-out and step back from the incestuous and self-fulfilling prophecy of impending doom?

> The world is moving in an entirely different direction from that of business.

The world is moving in an entirely different direction from that of business. Everything is speeding up while business is slowing down. It's a world of paradox and contradiction, in which up is down, down is up, macro is micro, micro is macro, global is local, local is global, big is small, and small is big.

Standing still on the treadmill of change can result in only one outcome: a crashing fall!

The new power structure rewards David and punishes Goliath. Size still matters, but not as the sense of entitlement. Amazon is huge. They own enough bricks and mortar to fill the Empire State Building three times over–only they invest in warehouses and fulfillment instead of legacy retail outlets and showrooms.

There is a new business model in play: the application of *better, cheaper, and faster* to the bottom-up approach of getting to scale. It's a panacea of the *reaggregation* of a million micro-moments of individual contributions, creations, investments, and purchases, from Kickstarter to GoFundMe to Glassdoor to Instagram. And when you add them up, you get Facebook's 2.27 billion active monthly users as of the third quarter of 2018 (of which 1.74 billion are on mobile).

So don't think for a nanosecond that size and scale don't factor into this equation. They can and they do, and to prove it, consider these two questions:

1. What happened to the companies that fell out of the Fortune 500?

2. Who took their place?

The answer to the former question is suckage.

The answer to the latter is startups, of course. They grew so quickly, no one saw them coming...or even if they did, there was nothing the slumbering giants could do about it.

DEATH BY A THOUSAND BUDGET CUTS

At one of my recent keynotes in the United States, I stood up in front of 150+ marketers and said, "If there is anyone in this room who hasn't had one budget cut, reorg, restructure, or change in C-Suite leadership within the past 12 months? Raise your hand, and I will work for you FOR FREE in perpetuity."

Risky move? Hardly. **Not one person raised their hand.**

Perhaps this was just a U.S. problem, so I asked a room filled with the *crème de la crème* of Belgian marketers how many of them had had a minimum of one of the aforementioned corporate life events over a 12-month timeframe.

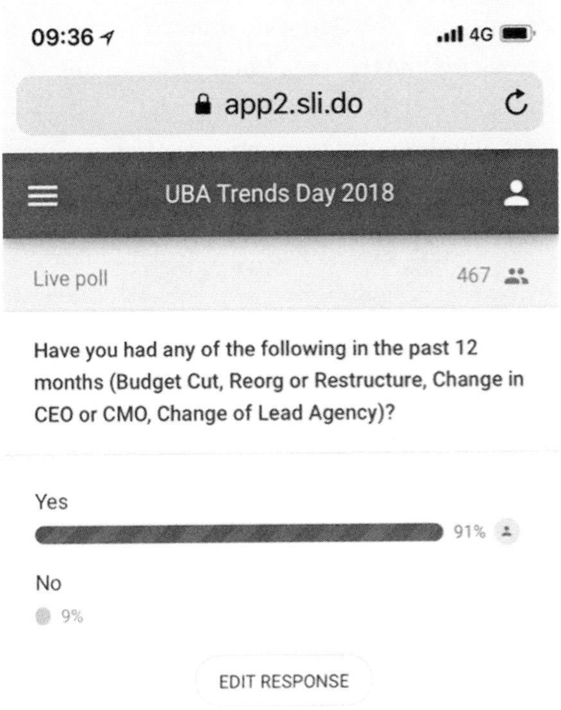

Figure 3.2 - CMO Poll

As you can see, 91 percent answered yes. I wasn't surprised by the number of people who responded in the affirmative. I was actually surprised that as many as 9 percent answered no! Regardless, 91 percent says it all, doesn't it?

How many of these "corporate life events" have *you* experienced over the past 12 months? And how many times?

Isn't it pathetic that we need a "click all that apply" or "all of the above" option to choose from?

Is it any wonder that corporations are struggling to keep up with their more nimble, agile competitors, from startups to market challengers? Think Jet Blue, Casper, Ally, or Monzo. There's no momentum in business today, because every single time a company gets their nose out in front, the rug is pulled out from under them by yet another hiring freeze, round of layoffs, or "pause button" on any new projects.

Whenever a new C-Suite executive is appointed, they immediately look to "get up to speed" by assessing all ongoing priorities and pending commitments. Unfortunately, "get up to speed" is basically a dirty euphemism for "not made here syndrome," and the kiss of death to anything and anyone associated with the previous/outgoing regime. The culmination of this discovery typically manifests itself in a mass firing of these inherited and therefore contaminated employees, as well as lead and partner agencies, vendors, or service providers with the same connection.

And, surprise, surprise—the newly-vacated internal executive roles and external partners are filled by a incestuous group of people and companies who worked with them in their previous job or role. Talk about nepotism and "draining the corporate swamp."

This scenario is the norm versus the exception. And it's shameful.

REORGS ARE THE DEVIL

When was the last time you had a successful restructure? They are really just overhead reduction wolves in change-management sheep's clothing. They tend to come from the (lame) brainchild of an external consultant, and almost always end up causing mass confusion, demotivation, and dysfunction.

Take forced rotation, for example. Why on earth would you continuously move people around, especially those who are less and less likely to stick around for the long haul? Why create an internal version of the external hell cited above? It used to be the case that in order to be a successful executive in a global multinational, one had to uproot one's family and literally trek around the globe to take up various positions on each major continent. Why? Why bother? Why is an American better equipped to run Asia-Pacific? Or a Brazilian best suited to take the reins of a North American concern?

I'll bet you there's a correlation between budget cuts, restructures, or reorgs and share price. Anyone care to wager?

My message is very simple: STOP! STOP the madness. STOP the short-termitis. STOP the musical chairs.

What business needs, now more than ever, is to be vested and invested in the long game. A unique mix of "insecure stability" or "secure instability," whichever way you cut it, is about finding a balance between momentum and continuity in the midst of a deeply disruptive, volatile, and ever-changing business environment.

When it comes to your organizational chart, I would recommend **issuing a moratorium on change**. I know it might sound like a giant contradiction to advocate against change, but in this case, I'm being serious. Anyone coming into a new position should be obliged to pick up the ball and run with it.

Instead of reinventing the wheel...why not just repurpose it? An incoming C-suite executive should be banned from changing—or even considering changing—the existing agency or partner structure for 12 months. Ironically, this is how much time is normally wasted doing the whole dog-and-pony show of audit, discovery, putting the business under review, and going through the whole RFI (request for information), RFP (request for proposal), and RFS (request for suckage) process.

Think about how much momentum is lost and how much time is wasted during this "transition," when the grand reveal is the hiring of the despot cronies who have to come to scrape the bottom of the barrel in order to please the procurement bean counters.

If corporations are an endangered species, then their leadership is under even more scrutiny, duress, and danger of being forced into unplanned, early retirement. According to executive recruitment firm Spencer Stuart, the average tenure of a CMO in 2017 was 44 months. Worse still, only 11 percent of marketing execs in top companies were African American, Hispanic, or Asian. About 28% were women.

If you know you are a ticking time bomb, why would you take 25-33 percent of your time to make what is essentially an utterly predictable, superficial, and impotent move? No tagline is going to be that good.

TIME IS THE ENEMY

The result of all of this change for the sake of change is waste. Wasted time. Wasted energy. Wasted momentum.

And the longer things stall in the holding pattern of procrastination and contrived wheel-spinning, the more likely they are to result in...you guessed it...another budget cut that NO ONE saw coming.

Dysfunction begets dysfunction, and this continuous one-step-back does not result in two steps forward, but rather another step back, or even a giant back-pedal.

So now your budget has been cut by 10 percent, and you are being told to reduce your spend. Instead of weeding out the old, tired, and stale, business seems to follow the L.I.F.O. methodology: last in, first out. In other words, the fresh, current thinking gets whacked at the expense of the same old, same old.

L.I.F.O. may be a generally-accepted accounting principle, but it sucks royally when it comes to innovation and staying competitive in these ever-changing times. Perhaps we should replace with L.I.F.O. with **L.I.P.O.** in order to cut out the fat!

BUDGET FOR INNOVATION

The 60/30/10 (or 70/20/10 variation) approach to innovation is widely known and lauded. At Google (a best-in-class practitioner of this operating philosophy), engineers are given 10 percent of their time to spend on things that have absolutely no direct connection to their business. The idea is to expand their minds, feed their passions, arouse their curiosity, and ultimately inspire diverse and fresh thinking.

Eric Schmidt, ex-Executive Chairman of Google and Alphabet, Inc., talks a lot about the tyranny of *incrementalism*, or thinking too small in a manner too contained. Tweaking the status quo will never, ever give way to breakthrough thinking. On the one hand, it is akin to a band-aid solution for a gaping wound. On the flipside, the metaphor of pissing against the wind comes to mind (don't try this in a moving car.)

Instead, Google utilized 10X thinking. Everything had to have a stretch component to it. Every goal needed to have an extra "zero" added to it. The rationale behind this was that with lofty expectations came lofty accomplishments.

Some corporates have tried to adopt this approach—most notably, The Coca-Cola Company with their "Now, New, Next" framework.

I'm not even sure Coca-Cola employs this practice anymore.

The good news is that more and more titles are cropping up with the word "innovation" in them. The bad news is that most of these people are pretty powerless. They are to innovation what digital directors were to online, circa 2001. Chained to musty, dusty, cobwebby broom closets, they are called upon anytime a vendor comes in with some kind of technology no one quite understands. They have no budget. No influence. No impact.

I divide this new class of professionals into three categories. Let's use the 60/30/10 rule as our rubric.

60 percent of them are full of shit.....I mean, bravado. They talk a big game, but are completely ineffective. They are not only stripped of budget; they are also *sans* credibility in their own organizations. They walk down the corridor, and everyone does a hard 180. I was probably in this category when I ran Interactive Media at the Madison Avenue agency TBWA\Chiat\Day.

Back in the day, I was writing weekly columns for one of the media trades, *MediaPost*. I was sitting on countless panels, talking up the vision behind online and the wave of disruption that was about to follow. Back at the agency, however, I was *persona non grata*.

I didn't take it personally. I was just like all my "fringy" (or cringy) counterparts at all the other agencies. That's why we needed our twice-yearly industry boon-doggles—to blow off steam with our own kind.

The real tragedy here is that NOTHING has changed. Interactive got replaced with social. Social got replaced with mobile. Mobile got replaced with whatever the hell is supposed to be the next big thing. Perhaps the only thing that has changed is the superficial lip service given to innovation by agencies and clients alike. I call this the *tinderfication of innovation*.

Any work done in the area of change is nothing more than a tactical check on the to-do list of nice to have toys, designed to appease whichever higher up is getting their knickers into a knot over the dogged insistence on the status quo. Old farts!

Then there's the 30 percent fighting the good fight. They mean well, and they do everything in their power to further the cause. They are forced to be scrappy, and in this respect, they are a startup within the belly of the beast. Unfortunately for them, there is no guarantee of funding on the immediate horizon. There is an acute sense of frustration with this group, as they have a pretty good idea of where the world is heading, but can't get any meaningful movement from within.

Perhaps I fell into this category instead...

THE BLUE LIGHT IS (NOT) BACK

When I was at TBWA/Chiat/Day in 2000/2001, I collaborated with an ex-Wall Street analyst on a pretty awesome (if I do say so myself) business idea for the discount retailer KMart.

In 2000/2001, CDs (for those born after 1980, that stands for compact discs) from AOL (for those born after 1980, that stands for America Online) were still all the rage, announcing, "You've got mail" behind their walled garden. Broadband Internet access had not quite hit critical mass. In fact, most people were still dialing up via modem (for those born after 1980...oh, forget it!) The Internet was still a largely mysterious and unknown factor.

Kmart as a brand was a follower, competing with other behemoths like Walmart. Target was beginning its inexorable march toward cheap chic.

Our idea was to dedicate a piece of real estate within a Kmart store to education, lectures, and the hands-on training associated with "getting online." This included themes or focus areas like privacy, parental controls, and protecting your kids online. Yes, even e-commerce was part of the syllabus. Group seminars would be free, and would take place during specific times of the week when store traffic was at its lowest (thereby creating "appointment viewing" during slow business hours). One-on-one or private lessons could be booked anytime with points based upon actual spend in the store (in other words, a loyalty mechanism based on actual purchases.)

Following me so far?

Naturally, relevant tech hardware, accessories, and services would be conveniently merchandised around this area. In addition, there would be an obvious halo effect—from people who might have come to Kmart specifically for the seminar—on incremental shopping.

We called it "Cyber Kafé," using the Kmart K, of course!

So, what become of this idea? Nothing. It never got a whiff of consideration.

I wish I could tell you it was because the agency's Kmart client passed on the idea, but the real tragedy is that the "suits" (aka client-service execs at the agency) didn't even put this in front of the executives at the retailer. As "guardians of the brand" or gatekeepers, their take was that Kmart customers were just not ready for this techie mumbo jumbo. "Come on, Joe, the average Kmart customer is not online, and those who are, are not exactly on broadband." They might even have used the words "dumb" and "poor," but my memory is foggy. My response was, "So let's help them get online...become more comfortable online...purchase more online."

Then there are the 10 percent of people who actually get things done. They find wins within the organization and merchandise them intelligently, both within and outside of the company.

B. Bonin Bough might have exhibited a healthy dose of self-importance, narcissism, and arrogance in his day (he was clearly on track to become Commander in Chief), but in his role as head of media at Mondelēz International, he created movement and the seeds of meaningful change.

Bough put a ludicrous ambition stake on the ground in 2013 when he decreed that Mondelēz would one day spend 10 percent of their entire media budget on mobile. He created an initiative called Mobile Futures, in which I was fortunate to play a leading role. Mobile Futures eventually morphed into Shopper Futures, and when the dust settled, it had deployed in North America, Brazil, Australia, and Germany.

So, what was the problem? The problem was that Bonin left Mondelēz in 2017, and not coincidentally, the Futures venture is now a thing of the past.

CHAPTER 4

DECONSTRUCTING SUCKAGE

CORPORATIONS SUCK. WE ESTABLISHED THAT IN THE PREVIOUS CHAPTER, BUT I'M not done yet. In this chapter, I'll focus on the people who work for them, and some of the dumb decisions they make. Moreover, I'll introduce two intertwined forces which, when combined, are responsible for sounding the corporate death knell: the startup and the Entrepreneurial Revolution.

I like to describe myself as the Robin Hood of modern-day marketing I steal from the rich and give to the poor.

I suppose a better word for "stealing" in the business context would be "optimization:" moving money from one budget to another, or reallocating within a single budget between various line items on a flowchart. This thought process follows a two-step methodology of efficiency (from less to more efficient) and effectiveness (from less to more effective).

OPTIMIZATION ITSELF IS FLAWED

The problem with this method is that:

1. It draws on what was done *last year* in order to predict or forecast what will be done *this year* or *next year*.

2. It is zero-sum. In absolute terms, this could be seen as rearranging the deck chairs on the Titanic versus rethinking the entire process altogether.

3. It does not allocate what should be given, but rather what is available.

4. It does not factor in potential lift or upside, but rather what can be definitively measured and/or proven.

5. The measurement methodology itself is out of date, inaccurate, or incomplete.

6. It does not really allow for new budgets or the creation of new line items on the flow chart.

7. When inevitable budget cuts appear, the "new" or "fringe" are oftentimes (and by oftentimes, I mean ALL the time) the first to go.

> It's funny how we refer to return on investment (ROI) as the foundation behind all marketing, sales, sponsorship, and customer service, and yet none of this is really INVESTMENT at all. We actually classify it as an expense. An investment is not short-term in nature. An investment is not campaign-based, unless it's an actual political campaign; and even then, 50 percent will be wasted.

RICH MAN, POOR MAN

The corporation is the rich man. The global enterprise. The multinational. The brand. It's Procter. And It's Gamble. Kimberly. Clark. It's General. It's Motors. It's both Coca and Cola. It's Telstra and Orange. Pfizer and Phillips.

In 2017, paid media advertising worldwide was $583.91 billion, according to *eMarketer*. That's just ad spend, and doesn't factor in a whole bunch of other expenditures, such as experiential or event marketing, customer service, relationship marketing, product development, in-store, or shopper.

So, how much of it is well-spent?

JOHN WANAMAKER WAS AN ENTREPRENEUR

Over 120 years ago, retailing pioneer John Wanamaker said, "Half my advertising is wasted; the only problem is that I don't know which half."

...but what if we could measure it? And what if it was way more than 50 percent? How would you justify *that* to your shareholders?

Today, we can (and absolutely do) measure our marketing activities, and somehow, we're still hiding behind numbers that are based upon outdated or questionable methodologies, faulty assumptions, and incomplete information.

It's probably time to stop referring to John Wanamaker and let him rest in peace, once and for all. Instead, let's rethink our budgets holistically, and then allocate them across three specific move-forward scenarios.

Action 1: Measure what is not working, and do less of it.

Action 2: Measure what is working, and do more of it.

Action 3: Find new ways to do things better, cheaper, and/or faster.

COMPANIES HAVE MORE MONEY THAN BRAINS

That's not an insult. If you work for a large corporation, you must be super smart. And talented. I'm sure you are a great dancer, as well, but can you say the same for those around you?

How many of these bearded hipsters will be on payroll at the end of the year?

Even if you have great retention rates amongst your talented workforce, you *still* have more money than brains. Literally. You are flush with budget (even though you often claim poverty), but your truly scarce resource is, has been, and always will be your people.

So, isn't it time to use those wonderful brains and think about better uses for all that money?

Corporations are being slammed from both sides right now. They're struggling to attract top-tier talent and hold onto their existing pool. Additionally, engaging and activating existing middle management with the knowledge, expertise, and skills they require to be successful remains challenging.

The commitment to continued education is conspicuously absent. It's another corporate catch-22/lose-lose scenario with respect to finding budget to justify the ROI associated with investing in employee development. On the one hand, it's patently obvious that ramping up skills in the emerging tech space is of paramount importance, but at the same time, why flush this money down the toilet when you know they won't stick around long enough to apply these skills to their day-to-day?

DAMNED IF YOU DO, AND DAMNED IF YOU DON'T.

Case in point: the aforementioned mixed-media festival SxSW. It's quite possibly one of the easiest ways to get your team in the stream of progress and commitment to change. For about 4-5 days (which includes a weekend), attendees immerse themselves in networking, conversation, debate, creative discourse, and Red Bull. It's a golden opportunity to inject your talent directly into the epicenter of disruption. The connection and inspiration opportunities are endless. And yet when I ask folks if I'll see them there, they shake their heads and mention their employers won't allow them to go without taking personal leave. Often, when I *do* see them there, they have actually had to pay their own way there! Pitiful!

The opposite end of the extreme is equally bad. In years past, some blue-chip elite have chosen to send their entire clown posse, descending on Austin like the plague with fire and fury, pomp and circumstance—a parade of posers. They have a rigid agenda that has been curated by an overpaid consultant, ripe with tons of free shit and VIP invites to parties from publishers and tech platforms looking to get into their professional pants. They miss the point completely in making organic, spontaneous, informal serendipity into nothing more than a glorified offsite.

Finding the best and brightest is hard enough. Keeping the best and the brightest takes that commitment to a whole new level.

THE LEAKY BUCKET OF CORPORATE SECURITY

You might think the divorce rate is high, but that's before you come face to face with the corporate divorce rate, which is a lot more disturbing.

Why would anyone coming out of college willfully choose to join a large company today versus going it alone? Pretty much every reason why this might have worked in the past has been marginalized or neutralized in recent times. Cutting your teeth and earning your spurs still has value and validity, to be sure, but there are multiple ways to leapfrog incumbent gates or checkpoints that represent credentials on a resume.

Training and development are no longer the pulls they once were, either, due to the continuous slashing of budgets—not to mention the fact that organizations are not exactly at the forefront of teaching employees the new skills they will need to be successful in the new economy and changing operating landscape.

Being a part of a company no longer guarantees job security. When industry after industry is falling victim to the steady advances of technology, automation, artificial intelligence, and/or the disruption of new entrants in the market, the only norm these days is yet another round of layoffs.

CASE IN POINT: FORRESTER PREDICTS 24.7 MILLION JOBS LOST TO AUTOMATION BY 2027

Between 2017 and 2027, that equates to a job loss of 17 percent. Fortunately, technology will also create 14.9 million new jobs over the next decade, with automation generating jobs equivalent to 10 percent of the workforce through 2027.

So, yes, some good news; but overall, a net loss in jobs—and let's not kid, the people losing their jobs are not exactly front-runners for these new roles, are they?

There are still plenty of workers who would rather choose the corporate devil over the startup angel. Either option comes with the very real possibility of job loss. The question is, to what degree do you want control over your own destiny versus putting all of your eggs in the talons of the human resources department?

Big Business has created a vicious cycle of marathon proportions, in which there are no winners except at the very top of the pecking order. It's like a giant Ponzi scheme. Think about it: the ultimate price (or prize) of incompetence at the C-suite level is to walk away with a golden parachute: being paid millions upon millions of dollars to get as far away from the company as possible. Doesn't seem fair at all.

When the dust settles after yet another round of musical chairs, the employees left standing are the real losers and collateral damage. They're almost immediately cut off at the knees, expected to pick up the slack of the dearly departed; thereby adding "overworked" to their LinkedIn description of "underpaid and underappreciated." Work-life balance goes out the window, as does motivation.

I have experienced this personally in my corporate experience, and it's one of the primary reasons I choose not to work in the corporate world anymore. My time is my time. It's the only time I have. It's limited. It's precious. You *don't* own me!

The corporation is apathetic at best, and cruelly manipulative at worst when it comes to honest and genuine commitment to the well-being of its employees. The scant few companies that buck this trend by being truly employee-centric (see Starbucks later in the book) are studied for their unique culture, but when did giving a damn become so exceptional that it became the exception to the norm?

Don't get me wrong—I'm all for corporate gyms, baby daycare, maternity/paternity leave, and the ability to work from home, but I think companies could and should do more. I'd like to see a massive overhaul of compensation, incentive schemes, and ownership. You know...like equity. The same equity you'll get from being part of a startup.

Happiness is good and all, but it doesn't pay the rent, now, does it?!

SAM WALTON, MEET OLIVER TWIST

Jay Chiat once said, "Let's see how big we can get before we suck," and that seems to be endemic to all major corporations that somehow lost their way and forgot that they were once startups themselves.

This quote was also the inspiration behind the title of the book.

Entrepreneurs are not restricted or defined by age, company size, or experience, but rather by cultural conditioning, passion, and purpose. It's ironic that when it comes to rewriting history, creating impact, and making real change, it's often assumed that the largest companies with the deepest pockets are best-equipped to deliver—and yet it is the startups that are tearing up the rulebooks and disrupting the status quo by demonstrating "lean" and hungry commitment to innovation, risk-taking, and agile business.

For now, let's think small and focus on the little guy. Let's talk about the fact that starting a business has never been so easy, and yet succeeding has never been so hard.

Low to virtually nonexistent barriers of entry have, to a certain extent, become part of the problem. When the lure and promise of hitting it big with the next WhatsApp, Snapchat, or Slack combines with the ease of developing a minimum viable product (MVP), it is no wonder that "founders" today are as abundant as Starbucks baristas. Most of these founders will be lucky to get a job as a barista, because luck will invariably not smile on them. They will almost certainly fail.

Seventy-five percent of venture-backed startups end up failing.[1] Other numbers put this as high as 90 percent. And yet, these astronomical failure rates don't stop dreamers from dreaming, inventors from inventing, and employees quitting their corporate jobs in favor of the startup life.

This book isn't designed to discourage entrepreneurs from starting a business. On the contrary; I'd like to see more people thinking and acting like founders. I'd like to see more corporations encouraging their employees to pitch their ideas to the internal corporate sharks. I'd also like to see more of these concerns succeed crazily.

There's an old saying: "Just because you can, doesn't mean you should." That's true, but it doesn't really apply anymore when it comes to looking toward technology to solve business, human, societal, environmental, or personal problems. If anything, it is *because* you can that you should. Of course, this doesn't mean checking sanity, common sense, strategic planning, and financial acumen at the door.

Our culture has become so risk-averse that we are paralyzed at the prospect of putting ourselves out there. What we need to do is take a chance, risk it all, and be prepared to fail.

I blame the corporation.

As I tell my son, "If you aren't prepared to take a risk and possibly fail, you never will fail; you will also never succeed." Why is it that we'd rather "not fail" than succeed? Why are we so afraid of a limited downside (which is ultimately quantified, measurable, and tangible in terms of time and cost) versus an unlimited upside (qualified in more intangibles, like competitive advantage, differentiation, viral success, and unicorn sightings?)

Sure we might fail, but there are a growing number of fearless explorers who can't get enough failure....

THE ENTREPRENEURIAL REVOLUTION

It takes a certain combination of curiosity, frustration, and masochism to become an entrepreneur. I like to use the Robert F. Kennedy quote to encapsulate this idea: "*There are those who see things and ask why; and then there are those who see things as they could be, and ask, 'Why not?'*"

I'm sure there are many studies, Myers-Briggs and Rorschach tests to quantify the prototypical entrepreneur, but in actuality, anyone can start a company these days. Some of the time, they're actually entrepreneurs; at other times, they simply end up being entrepreneurs.

The world has changed, and it continues to change at a radically and increasingly disruptive pace. Yet this change is actually quite reassuring in its predictability and inevitability. It's kind of like the final scene in the movie *Deep Impact*, when the tidal wave is hurtling toward the Hamptons and Tea Leoni is on the beach in the arms of her father, completely at peace.

From a business standpoint, we've probably witnessed several changes that have had "deep impact" on our professional and personal lives.

1. **The Industrial Revolution**: the transition to new manufacturing processes in the period from about 1760 to sometime between 1820 and 1840.

2. **The Creative Revolution**, which took place predominantly in New York the late 1950s and into the 1960s and was led by people with names like Bernbach and Burnett. You probably know them better by their *Mad Men* fictional names: Draper, Sterling, and Olsen.

3. **The Digital Revolution**, also known as the Third Industrial Revolution[2] according to Wikipedia, covered a period of time that began around the turn of this century and saw the mainstreaming of digital.

4. Now witness the dawn of the Forth or the **Entrepreneurial Revolution**, from the time commencing with the founding of Facebook, Twitter, YouTube, the launch of the iPhone, and, of course, Nextflix, Uber, AirBnB, Tesla, and the like.

Millennials may dominate the startup scene today, but that doesn't make the entrepreneurial revolution a young person's game, nor does it mean they'll stay young forever. This has far-reaching implications when it comes to the motivations determining WHY people start companies and WHAT their end game or exit strategy might be....

Also worth noting: a revolution is not one-sided. There is always an enemy, and often, said enemy is defeated. Think digital versus analog. In this case, the Entrepreneurial Revolution may very well come at the expense–and fall–of the Corporate Era.

ENTREPRENEURS RULE O.K.^{BETA}

Have you ever been to a shared workspace like WeWork in the U.S., Dreamplex in Ho Chi Minh, Vietnam, the Ministry of New in Mumbai, or Runway East in Shoreditch, London?

You'll witness an incredible band of brothers and sisters representing scores of businesses, business plans, startups, and ideas. You'll meet ordinary people with extraordinary ideas about how to change the word. You'll observe a hive-like frenzy of activity. This will result in strangers helping other strangers with common problems, and in this networking dance, connections will be made, bonds formed, and problems solved.

The Entrepreneurial Revolution is not a free-for-all (and I mean that both in terms of chaos versus order and free versus fee.) At the early end of the spectrum, startup launch programs and accelerators like The Founder Institute are helping aspiring entrepreneurs put the initial building blocks together to create the foundation necessary for the road that lies ahead.

The Founder Institute is a program that runs quarterly and is now in over 200 cities, corresponding to 60 countries and six continents. It has led to an estimated 25,000+ new jobs being created and an estimated portfolio value of over $20 billion. Programs take place during the week at night, and help guide budding founders through lessons including Naming & Vision, Legal, Growth, and Equity & Funding. Pretty much all of these people have day jobs, and almost all of them are counting down the days to when they can give their employer the middle finger before their employer gives them a pink slip.

IF YOU CAN'T BEAT 'EM, BORE 'EM

To be fair, corporations have tried to tap into the entrepreneurial revolution. They've encouraged jeans-wearing, introduced casual Fridays, and even brought about the 4-day workweek. They have standing desks, and occasionally let a dog wander through the office. Plus the obligatory beanbag and Ping-Pong table for aesthetic pleasure.

Not many of them have free food, though. It's a real pet peeve of mine to see companies charging their employees for food in their cafeterias. Yes, they may be subsidized, but the food tastes more like a Michelin tire than a Michelin star. It's not just the right thing to do, it makes good business sense: keep your employees nourished and energized to be more productive!

The reality is that even with free food, there isn't much a corporation can do to deliver the kind of complete experience (don't make me say the C word.... culture) that is both magnetic and magical. Corporations are deathly ill. They're sick to their stomachs, and the only cure is twofold: more cowbell, and more entrepreneurial spirit.

People want meaning. They want to believe in something greater than themselves. They crave the opportunity to dare. They are curious and mischievous... or at least they were when they were younger, or before they sold their souls to the corporate devil.

Slowly but surely, a global awakening of epic proportions is taking place, and it's enough to make the founders of these corporations turn in their graves. They were all entrepreneurs. It was Walt Disney who said, "If you can dream it, you can do it." Today, Disney chief Bob Iger says inspirational things like, "Our plan on the Disney side is to price this (new streaming service) substantially below where Netflix is." *Zzzzzzz.*

Mickey, Donald, and Goofy are shaking their heads right now (or using the hashtag #smh).

TO THE VICTORS GO THE SPOILS

Increasingly, able-bodied workers are opting for the hurly-burly world of the startup.

> "Joining a startup with all its dysfunction, instability, uncertainty, and insecurity is all part of the experience, and it is that experience which holds more sway over the oasis mirage of corporate (dys)function."

Put differently, joining a startup with all its dysfunction, instability, uncertainty, and insecurity is all part of the experience, and it is *that* experience which holds more sway over the oasis mirage of corporate (dys)function.

Opting for the masochism of the startup world over the sadism of the corporate world seems like a no-brainer of a choice, when you think about it.

A TRAGIC TWIST?

An article published in 2017 asked, "Is the golden age of startups over?" It cited the new Big 5—no, not the game reference of lion, elephant, buffalo, leopard, and rhino, but rather Amazon, Apple, Google, Facebook, and Microsoft—and how they are truly dominating (and even monopolizing) the markets for technology, talent, funding, and more.[3] Startups today are finding it increasingly hard to identify a clear path to growth—even more so when they rely on the infrastructure and platforms of the Big 5 to succeed. This creates a precarious position in which any of the Big 5 can, at any time, essentially shut them down—explicitly, with a cease-and-desist, or more subtly, by just changing the algorithm.

So yes, perhaps the new class of startups does need to update their exit forecasts to eliminate going public or becoming a unicorn (less than 1% will), and instead just say, "to be bought by Google." There are worse outcomes, for sure. In addition, there will always be speculative opportunities whereby startups can zig when the Big 5 zag. The article cites three such use cases: 1) speed as a premium; 2) deep delivery on niche areas; or 3) gray areas that may or may not be legal!

Buyer beware, but even with this known risk, it's still worth it.

DON'T START WITH WHY. START WITH WTF???!!!!

Corporations simply, positively, absolutely, and most definitely need to jettison all the clichés, bullshit bingo, and ephemeral crap about purpose, big ideas, storytelling, content strategy, hackathons, or whatever the fad of the month is in order to focus on only one thing, and one thing only: survival. Without the ability to feed, nurture, and strengthen the lifeblood of companies, talent, growth, longevity, and ultimately survival are all compromised—and are increasingly under tremendous (and, arguably, insurmountable) pressure.

CHEATING DEATH

Without question, the key to your salvation lies in the heart of the startup cult and culture. Getting back in touch with corporate roots can lead to a reincarnation or rebirth of sorts, transporting a company back to a time when they moved more quickly, failed faster, took more risks, and were more agile, openminded, scrappy, hungry, flexible, and fierce.

Let's be honest; this isn't going to happen overnight, and in reality, it's most likely not going to happen at all—but that doesn't mean it's impossible, and it doesn't mean you should give up.

Do I think large companies can succeed in terms of becoming more start-up-like? In a word: no. In two words: hell, no!

Which won't stop them from issuing press releases about being "the world's largest startup." Tom Paradis created a more irreverent rebuke:

- If you have been working at your company for a month and you still don't know everyone's name, you might not be a startup.

- If you can afford to take out numerous ads on national television, you might not be a startup.

- If your head of HR says, "We try to create a culture that is a like a startup," you might not be a startup.

You get the picture!

SECTION 2:

CROSSROADS

CHAPTER 5

TAKING RESPONSIBILITY

W HY WOULD ANYONE WILLINGLY INFLICT PAIN ON HIM- OR HER-SELF? To you or me, that might indicate a degree of insanity—and yet masochism is not exactly an outlier behavior, is it?

I can recall many times I've offered something to a friend, saying, "Smell this, it's disgusting!" And more than once, the friend obliged. According to a *National Geographic* blog piece, the psychological motivation behind the appeal of stinky things is the same as the appeal of roller coasters, painfully spicy foods, and deep-tissue massage. Likewise with reading sad novels or watching scary movies. So, what's the common thread?

Paul Rozin, PhD, Professor Emeritus of Psychology at the University of Pennsylvania, coined the term *benign masochism* to describe the way humans enjoy negative sensations and emotions when they're reassured no harm will come to them. Like your mate passing you a Trinidad Moruga Scorpion or Carolina Reaper chili, saying, "Taste this."

It doesn't take a doctoral degree in psychology to "unpack" or dissect why humans do incredibly dumb things. It could be because they are dumb. Or it could be the masochistic fetish, which would explain doing dumb things intentionally in order to inflict pain on oneself...and/or on others.

This is what appears to happen between the hours of 9 and 5, from Monday to Friday in the corporate world.

It has produced the kinds of howlers that have become staples in any MBA program or textbooks—hallmarks of "what not to do," or worst practices. Things like:

- New Coke

- Mars, Inc. turns down the opportunity for M&Ms to be the candy luring E.T. from his hiding place, thereby clearing the way for Hershey's Reese's Pieces.

- IBM, in what may be considered a massive misunderstanding of where the digital world was heading, allowing Microsoft to retain the copyright for its DOS platform.

The problem, as the saying goes, is that if you point your finger, there are three pointing back at you! The *real* challenge is to understand the reasons *why* we make these decisions in the first place.

The answer is NOT that we are dumb. We are smart. Incredibly smart. We have studied. We have graduated. We do incredibly well playing armchair quarterback at *Wheel of Fortune* or *Jeopardy*, but when we swipe our ID badge or punch into our corporate jail cells, something overcomes us with an acute case of dumbness.

Smart people making dumb decisions.

DR JEKYLL AND MR. CXO

I struggled with this apparent contradiction between how people think (smart) and how we act (dumb). At first, my conclusion was that people are schizophrenic.

Or perhaps it is extremely willful. Premeditated. Calculated. Are these decisions based solely upon preserving the status quo and corporate-ladder hierarchy? Hypocrisy is nothing new to us. We see it in politics. We see it in life.

We see it in business. But why? Is it the fear of change combined with bravado as the ultimate built-in defense mechanism? Or just a safety blanket of comfort to fall back on when times get tough?

We see this behavior exhibited abundantly in the C-Suite, most notably by the chief marketing officer. The larger the organization, the less power they seem to wield. They hold external influence in the industry, but internally, they are really just cheerleaders. They address a room filled with their industry peers, who are all in on the dirty joke.

Perhaps you've been in the audience at a big-time conference listening to a chief marketing officer lambasting the industry, lamenting the lack of creativity and innovation, challenging the market to bring fresh and disruptive ideas and declaring themselves open for business....only to be utterly disappointed when you cartwheel your way to the front of the line, present your business card, enthusiastically and passionately deliver your pitch, and hear, "Go talk to my agency!"

The explanation is quite simple: follow the money. The real money (depending on the organization) resides within budgets or P&Ls that belong to individual countries, regions, business units, or brands. "Corporate" becomes nothing more than impotent or glorified spokespeople. The words *global* and *corporate* (and don't forget *innovation* from earlier) in a business title telegraph futility.

One line item they *do* control is the selection of advertising agencies, which is perhaps why they so gleefully sink their gums into the agency search as one of the first orders of business. It's not that they think this is their number-one priority; it's just that it's the only arena in which they can actually affect change.

It's also the reason why their job tenure continues to drop....

This corporate condition is not limited to the marketing department. Even the mighty CEO can be limited and hamstrung in terms of green-lighting projects that may step on the toes of their fellow executives or direct reports. When a CEO cannot green-light a project and needs to hand it down the food chain, sorry to tell you, but it's probably not going to happen at all....

SOLITARY CONFINEMENT

No doubt, there are some bad eggs out there. Bad actors. Badly behaved people. Miscreants only in it for themselves. No doubt, there are those intent on rocking any boat, as long as it isn't theirs.

We know these people are smart. I'd also like to believe they're good. At our core, aren't we all good?

At an individual level, don't we all want the same things? We all want to be good. Do good. Make the world a better place. Be better spouses, parents, friends, and coworkers.

Individuals are born to create; to innovate. You or I might not be a born leader, but we can always aspire to become one. We are seekers of the truth. Solvers of problems. Always in search of a better way forward.

The quote at the beginning of this book reminds us that the human race has survived and thrived by adapting to change. This is the essence of evolution. We still have this primal gift or talent, only it has been so severely repressed within us that I fear it might be too late to awaken the instinct of survival, which is needed now more than ever before.

I HAVE SEEN THE ENEMY, AND THE ENEMY IS THE CORPORATION

The very nature, structure, and makeup of the corporation makes *smart people make dumb decisions*. This is due to a cocktail of lethargy, organizational dysfunction, risk aversion, siloed mentality, politics, slow and conservative thinking, procrastination, tradition or bad habits, and an overall inability to adjust to market conditions.

The systems, processes, and guardrails that were once built to last, today are built to suck. If a company doesn't take care of its people, why should they take care of the company? Left to their own devices, employees are going to pocket a boatload of Post-its, Sharpies, and printer paper and sell them on eBay!

The systems that once supported the growth of the corporation have now becomes a cancer that is destroying the very competitiveness of the enterprise.

There are exceptions, but they are few and far between. These are the fast followers, but they are followers nonetheless. They are still lagging behind their consumers and falling further and further beneath the cruel and unforgiving sands of time.

IN THE LAND OF THE BLIND...

...the one-eyed man is king. Only in this scenario, it is the blind leading the blind. Corporations are benchmarking themselves against themselves; against their traditional competitors; and against the usual suspects. They are content to jostle or jog for position within a faceless pack. No one wants (or needs) to stick out his/her neck for fear of it being chopped off by a basement-dwelling blogger, disgruntled customer, or fake news.

Corporations are blinded by the bright and shiny light of fads, or whatever the hell *The Wall Street Journal* says they should be preoccupied with. They are so obsessed with keeping up with the Joneses, they don't see what's coming down the pike. Beware the Anglerfish of nice-to-have false promises and hype.

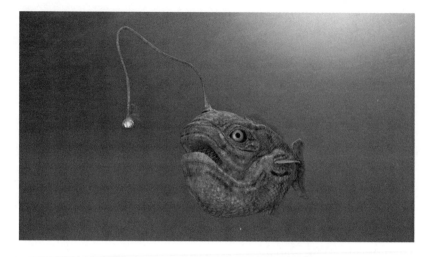

Figure 5.1 - Beware Bright and Shiny Lights

My resolution to this apparent contradiction became obvious. People are not schizophrenic at all. We are smart, but we have been held back and held down by the bureaucracy of large corporations. Our brilliant minds are being wasted; lost in a labyrinth of routine, neutered by a lack of ability to push through innovative ideas, new concepts, and creative or disruptive business models.

We are not powerless, either; to the contrary. We are all superheroes capable of limitless potential, figuring out how to break free from our corporate kryptonite.

FIX THE CORPORATION (OR KILL IT)

If individuals are not the problem, surely all we need to do is fix the corporation? Move some money around. Create a new budget or two. Make some tweaks to the org chart with a combination of boxes and dotted/solid lines. Maybe even make up a new title or two (might I suggest chief survival officer?)

If only it were that simple. And don't think I didn't check myself at the suggestion of solving this with yet another reorg (because that's what it would entail.)

Perhaps the problem is that we've given the "individuals" in question a free pass. Perhaps they are not the innocent victims they claim to be. Perpetuating the status quo has *become* the status quo among people with too much to lose by "unlearning" their bad habits in order to reboot and start again. It gets even more futile and desperate when they combine to form groups (committees, working groups, task forces, departments, boards).

No one is more at fault than old white guys. Corporations are riddled with them, and it sucks to say this, because I am old, white, and male (but fortunately, I'm incredibly immature.)

The median age of S&P 500 directors today is 63. Ten years ago, it was 61. There are 71 directors who are at least 80 years old. Just 28 directors are under 40. CBS's 14-member board is one of the oldest. Four of its directors are at least 80, and the youngest, 61. I guess this is what happens with Les Moonves is your spirit animal.

So what does your Board look like? Or does it closer resemble the word "bored" when it comes to dynamism, decisiveness and diversity?

How about the last conference you attended? Did women and people of color make up 50 percent of the panelists and speakers? How about 5 percent? Given how diverse the population is, it isn't surprising that corporations are struggling to serve them.

For what it's worth, lack of diversity is just as much of a problem in the tech and startup arenas. It begins at school, and focuses on the critical area of S.T.E.M. (Science Technology Engineering Mathematics), or, as it is now called, S.T.E.A.M., with the A for Arts. Immigration holds a key for redemption, but sadly, it has become a political minefield.

Forced retirement is a euphemistic way of saying, "Let those old bastards die, already." As fun and flippant as it may seem to wish ill on the aging, mature end of the continuum, it's also inappropriate and actually inaccurate. I believe ageist views are extremely myopic. I've seen miraculous transformations occur when "mature" executives have wriggled free of their corporate shackles. Liberated from all the bullshit, they suddenly become the coolest people in the room, with bold, avant-garde ideas that are filled with delectable risk...as well as the risqué.

Turns out they were believers all along.

Turns out this isn't about age at all. It's about mindset.

The only pity is why they couldn't enact some of this thinking when they had budget, authority, and influence.

And so, the message is clear: make your choice, and make it today. Look around you at the next status meeting. At least one of you will be gone within the next six months. As in the movie *Rounders*, look for the sucker at the table, and if you can't see one, get up and leave, because the sucker is you.

Or maybe instead of *sucker*, consider *suck-ee*. As in, perhaps *you* are the reason for the suckage; the impediment to change. If you and your cronies are the ones holding back your company, then consider yourself served. You are on notice. Your days are numbered. You can hide behind the veil of politics for only so long before you are exposed for your ineptitude.

As the adage goes, people rise to the level of their own incompetence.

So, are you ready to take a stand?

Are you ready to make a change?

BREAK FREE. BREAK THE CYCLE.

If you've ever watched an episode of *Star Trek: The Next Generation* and their nemesis, the Borg, you would know that resistance is futile. And yet, resist we must in order to survive.

The corporate *Prime Directive* is all about survival. This is not a right. It is a privilege. We need to fight for it. Earn it. Every day.

The next few chapters will clear the way and provide a path forward.

CHAPTER 6

THE JOURNEY TO SURVIVAL

When you come to a fork in the road...

...take it.

If I don't quote the late legendary Yankees catcher and captain Yogi Berra at least once in every one of my books, I would feel remiss in my duty to state the obvious as eloquently and awkwardly as he did in his lifetime.

The message is simple: do something! Make a decision. Act. Now. Or. Else.

The writing is on the wall, and it doesn't look good for any business entity whose stock in trade lies in the past. Try this exercise on for size: if you had to unpack your company's secret sauce (competitive advantage, differentiation, barriers to entry or exit, patents, efficiencies, network, etc.), how much of it would be grounded in the past (history), present (operational excellence), as opposed to the future (mystery)?

As the saying goes: *Learn from the past, live in the present, and plan for the future.* Unfortunately, too many companies are living in the past, ignoring the present, and, in doing so, are almost certain to be denied a future.

The aforementioned 60/30/10 methodology works nicely with respect to investing in the "next" of now/new/next, but this implies that some kind of functional and productive foundation is in place upon which to experiment or dabble in innovation. When one applies the filter of past, present, and future, it seems woefully inept to budget and prioritize only 10 percent of your human and financial resources on the world—not as it was, not as it is, but as it is going to be.

To illustrate this point, here are a few anecdotal examples.

Let's begin with McDonald's.

If you've watched the movie *The Founder*, you should be able to respect the gumption, intensity, and lack of scruples of Ray Croc. It's a fairytale story of a desperate door-to-door salesman and how he built one of the greatest (if not THE greatest) franchises in history. It is story about the entrepreneurial spirit. It is the American story.

> **RAY KROC:** What is this?
>
> *Horford stares at the burger.*
>
> **JACK HORFORD:** It appears to be a hamburger.
>
> **RAY KROC:** It's not a McDonald's hamburger.
>
> He lifts off the bun, pointing out
> its myriad deficiencies.
>
> Too much ketchup. Three pickles, not two.
> Lettuce. Lettuce.

The McDonald's playbook is surgical, meticulous, uniform, systemized, itemized, and standardized to the decimal point. Walk into a McDonald's in Red Square, and you'll get the same product as in Rome (both Illinois and Italy).

Would you say that this is a company of the future? A company positioned to create the future? A company that has a future? My unscientific guess is that Mickey D's probably scores something like this: 40% (past), 50% (present) and 10% (future).

McDonald's is big, bad, and ugly enough to dabble in the unknown without risking it all.

They are currently rolling out self-service, touchscreen kiosks, and while it's novel to drag a tomato onto my bun, following the path of previous greasy fingers containing traces of fecal bacteria[1] (*ewww*), is this the kind of bold move that will ensure survival in a world turning away from fast food? How are they coping with new entrants—particularly those adjusting to radical lifestyle shifts and trends associated with health and wellness? How are they dealing with more aggressive, direct competitors like Domino's, who have been experimenting with pretty advanced omni-channel ordering, loyalty, alternative distribution channels, emerging technology, and more?

Have you seen the McDonald's mobile app? You're not missing anything. Store locator. Coupons and discounts. Nutritional Information. Seriously?

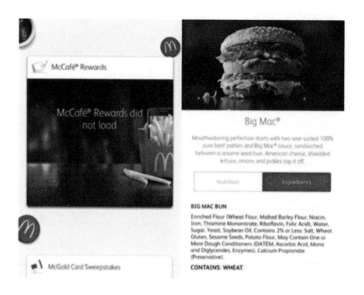

Figure 6.1 - McStoneAge

How does a company this big—and with such deep pockets—put out a mobile app that looks like it's stuck in a time warp from years back? It actually makes complete sense, as most branded apps are only missing the letters *cr* before the word *app*....

In the example above, clearly, the only "reward" is the disclosure about how unbelievably unhealthy a Big Mac is.

Fortunately for McDonald's, their stock price still reflects a reality in which fast food is both a guilty pleasure and a necessary evil, but there *will* come a day when neither of these conditions holds true anymore. When this day comes, the neon flicker of life in the golden arches will no longer illuminate over 99 billion sold.

Now let's trek east of Illinois to Detroit Motor City. A city razed by the credit crisis/mortgage meltdown recession that has struggled to recover. Detroit used to be synonymous with the automotive industry and the notable big three: Ford, General Motors, and whatever the hell the third one is called now.

Henry built Ford on the back of the then-innovative Model T. Customers could order any color they wanted, as long as it was black!

These days, Ford purchases 90 seconds of airtime during the Super Bowl to protest that *they are so much more than a car company*, citing ride-sharing, electric vehicles, bike-sharing, and self-driving cars as part of their pitch.

More on that later...but for this exercise, let's focus on General Motors. If you've visited Detroit, you may have seen the Marriott Renaissance Hotel, with the mighty blue-and-white GM logo on its masthead. Back in the day, General Motors meant more than any of the individual brands it housed. GM was as American as apple pie. If GM did well, America did well.

But that was in the past.

Today, GM has invested $500 million in the ride-sharing app Lyft. They have Maven—their response to Zipcar that allows people to pick up and drop off any GM car across a footprint of garages in selected markets. They announced going "all electric," with at least 20 vehicles projected to be in the electric lineup by 2023.

They also announced at the end of 2018 that they were laying off 15 percent of salaried workers, halting production at five plants in the U.S. and Canada, and, most significantly, ceasing production of the Cadillac CT6, XTS, Buick LaCrosse, Chevrolet Cruze, Impala, and Volt.

I would put General Motors at a 40 percent/40 percent/20 percent split between past, present, and future, which you might think is pretty progressive. As evidenced by its current predicament, it's not nearly progressive enough.

So, what's the ideal split? Obviously, it's going to vary from company to company and from industry to industry. I will tell you, though, where to begin: my opening gambit is a recommended even split of 33 percent/33 percent/33 percent...and take it from there.

33 PERCENT OF YOUR BUSINESS SHOULD HONOR THE PAST

This represents the <u>best</u> parts of your history, equity, and culture.

For Disney, this will always be the Mouse. For Apple, it's Steve. For Nike, it's the iconic swoosh.

It also requires a rejection of the worst parts of your history, equity, and culture (or lack thereof). Over the years, KFC has seemed to swing back and forth on the pendulum of distancing themselves from the *fried* part of Kentucky Fried Chicken versus doubling down on it and their creepy founder, Colonel Sanders (I have to imagine he's on some sex offender database somewhere...allegedly).

A GLIMMER OF HOPE FOR BRANDING

There is no question that branding, or brand marketing, has created brand powerhouses. This is like the "ribbon" (as it is referred to internally) associated with Coca-Cola. In many cases, brand equity has very tangible equity in terms of value on a balance sheet. Microsoft's acquisition of LinkedIn is represented on their balance sheet, for example.

There is no question that brands have value, and that brand-building creates value. With that said, **there is no question (zero doubt) that the way brands will be built over the next 20 years will be *very* different from the way they have been built over the past 20 years.** What this means is that every single company needs to be able to selectively "pick" elements from their brand archive that will stand the test of time, "purge" the deadwood, and "prune" accordingly in terms of adapting, updating, and evolving.

IN THE BEGINNING

Never forget where you've come from. The past should serve as a constant window to the future, especially when it stands as a reminder of humble beginnings, entrepreneurial sparks and epiphany, hunger, passion, intensity, scrappiness, and refusal to fail.

Henry Ford converted the storage shed behind his family's rented duplex at 58 Bagley Avenue in Detroit into a workshop. Would you be surprised to learn that so many of the world's largest companies started similarly—in garages?

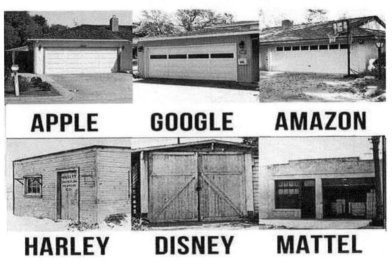

Figure 6.2 -Humble Beginnings

Sadly, today, the humility that was once present has been replaced with selective memory, arrogance, hubris, and dogmatic stubbornness.

The quick-service restaurant Denny's was going through a turnaround effort, and just when they were about to undertake the labor- and time-intensive project of discovering their purpose, they realized it had been in front of them all along. Harold Butler started Denny's in 1963, and was often quoted as saying, "I love to feed people." It was this statement that helped Denny's reconnect with its audience and *rediscover* its purpose. It also perfectly illustrates my point that companies need to get back to their humble beginnings.

Figure 6.3 - Denny's REdiscovers Its Purpose

33 PERCENT OF YOUR BUSINESS SHOULD BE DEDICATED TO THE PRESENT

Don't knock what you can't afford. Operational efficiencies that offer competitive advantages are integral to success.

If this book makes any point (over and over again), it's the importance of taking an initial extreme position in order to ultimately arrive at a position of balance and equilibrium.

The rise of private equity and consultants obsessed with driving down costs with an endless supply of scalpel and hatchet cuts are an important part of business, and clearly, there is merit in eliminating inefficiencies. This same group is also a major contributor to corporate rot.

I once met a genius of a man. To protect his identity, we'll call him Len Hause. Actually, his name *is* Len Hause, and he doesn't need protecting.

Len told me there are two types of people: numerator and denominator people. You'll probably get it immediately, but just in case, I'll explain: numerator people are focused on top-line growth—maximizing the unlimited upside, if you will. Denominator people are geared around the bottom line—specifically, minimizing all costs and expenses. So, which one are you? You'll probably say you're a numerator person, but you'd be lying, wouldn't you?

I used to think it was a binary choice, but again, it's about a healthy mix of both.

So if 33 percent of your time, effort, energy, budget, and talent is focused on operational excellence, that's just fine and dandy, as long as it stops there.

Another key component of the gift of the present is your customer. Operational excellence in a technologically ubiquitous, artificially intelligent and enlightened time presents both a blessing and a curse to the corporation. Blessed if you deliver. Cursed if you don't. Arguably, it has become a price of entry in the hearts, minds, and pocketbooks of the demanding customer with extremely high standards.

A chain is only as strong as its weakest link. Similarly, a company is only as strong as its weakest customer connection. Consider your most recent transaction, for it may be your last. Consider each interaction as if it were your only transaction. Consider each customer as if they were your only customer.

If you're wondering where to invest your "present," look no further than Starbucks for direction. Everything inside and outside the store is designed to *carpe latte*: from mobile ordering that minimizes lines and wait time to an app that utilizes "shake to pay" to create a paperless, plastic-less, seamless experience.

Starbucks takes a customer-centric (as opposed to corporate-centric) approach to realize operational efficiencies that create a self-fulfilling cycle of growth for the company.

33 PERCENT OF YOUR CORPORATE OXYGEN MUST BE FOCUSED ON THE FUTURE

What is the future? Let's wax philosophical for a moment. The future is not a mirror of the past. In fact, it's the direct opposite of the past. No more predictable business as usual. Want a highly unscientific smell test to make this slightly less ephemeral? Start in the present. Has your business changed substantially compared to 25 years ago? How about 10 years? 5 years? Less than 5 years ago? If the answer is yes, then it's a lock that the future will look NOTHING like it does today.

If that sounds scary, imagine if you had answered no!

Either way, if you recognize that the future is uncertain, you can put yourself into a position to affect change, which will continue to occur at an accelerated rate and within a compressed time frame.

Take the marketing holding company WPP, for example.

WPP was founded as Wire and Plastic Products Ltd. to manufacture wire shopping baskets in 1971. In 1986, WPP became the parent company of Picquotware, a manufacturer of teapots and jugs based in Northampton. In November 1987, a fire destroyed the Northampton factory, and production was restarted at Burntwood in Staffordshire. On 25 November 2004, WPP closed the Burntwood factory and stopped manufacturing Picquotware; all assets were sold on 14 December 2004.[1]

The company may have since made some (arguably) forced marches toward digital and automation, but has it changed enough? And quickly enough? According to numerous articles and earnings reports, the answer is unequivocally no. Its lunch is being stolen by the very same tech giants—like Facebook or Google—that it ironically funds (the curious case of the *frenemy*). On the strategic side of the business, it's not faring any better, with management consultancies like Accenture and Deloitte monopolizing upstream influence and critical decision-making.

Where does WPP need to be 10 years from now, if it is to survive? Where does it need to be five years from now? It is not a stretch to predict a scenario in which the (once) big fish of WPP is inevitably swallowed up by one of these tech or consulting companies.

I would have asked WPP's global CEO, Sir Martin Sorrell, for his split between past, present, and future—but he is no longer at the helm of the holding company (for reasons outside of job performance). To add insult to injury, he has now formed his own holding company, S4 Capital, which is essentially disintermediating his old business!

All's fair in suck and war!

WPP is no better or worse than the other holding companies in their space. There has already been a substantial amount of consolidation and M&A activity in this sector, and one thing is sure: the threat to WPP and its me-too doppelgangers will not come from one another, but from everyone and everywhere else. Rumors are rife with respect to some of its competitors being acquired.

In a world dominated by technology, it's like the central theme of *Lord of the Rings*: one ring to rule them all! How many viable competitors do Facebook, Apple, Amazon, or Google have? When everyone is scrapping for survival, it becomes a free-for-all melee.

And if necessity is the mother of invention, then it is from that manic chaos that true disruption is born—but not without a lot of pain first.

How can you not invest up to—or even more than—33 percent of your budget in this beautiful and delicious chaos?

THE ROAD TO RECOVERY

The first sign of recovery begins with admitting there's a problem. Without the buy-in of an addict, any changes are going to be extremely limited in terms of efficacy, and are likely to be short-lived, regardless.

For you, rehab is not an option. You don't have the luxury to detox by checking in to a facility. You're likely "checked out" already, which is part of the problem.

Nor is intervention an option. That's because you have no friends. The people around you are either complicit in terms of enabling the bad behavior in the first place, or waiting patiently on the sidelines to claim your Aeron chair when you get whacked—or, should I say, "retire to spend more time with your family."

Your recovery needs to be "on the job." You have to multitask or parallel-path in terms of finding the balance between past/present/future, but also in terms of reconciling short-term wins (getting that "W" on the board; hitting your earnings), medium-term milestones (optimization and reconciliation on budget, market share, and KPIs) and long-term gains (strategic priorities; competitive advantage).

The changes that are required are not small. They are not incremental tweaks, but at the same time, you do need to get those wheels of change moving. They have been dormant for too long, and they are corroded. It's time to grease those wheels and (re)ignite the engine of growth.

A SIMPLE 2X2 MATRIX

The road to recovery is grounded in action. Talking about change is great, but it is not enough.

In the spirit of K.I.S.S. (keep it simple, stupid), this is a stupidly easy way of auditing or taking stock in real time of your current investment level as it relates to your active budgets and a reframe of your past/present/future segmentation:

	OLD	NEW
ACCEPT the best of...	Universal Truths	Experimentation
REJECT the worst of...	"Insanity"	The Next Big Thing Syndrome (TNBT)

The matrix is grounded in equilibrium. This is not about an absolute or extreme rejection of the status quo. Nor is it a blind "all-in" embrace of bright and shiny objects, but rather a strategic and balanced mix of the following:

1. **The best of the old.** Universal or timeless truths are just that. Best practices grounded in irrefutable, consistent results should always be the foundation of any business. This includes a company's entrepreneurial roots, and specifically, the raison d'être and culture of the business itself. It also includes my gimp, advertising, and (even more so) direct-response or performance advertising. Based upon my purchase history on Instagram, I love buying useless products from China! I guess I'm open to being surprised and delighted, and I certainly enjoy the occasional (okay, frequent) impulse purchase. There's still room for advertising.

2. **The worst of the old.** Yes, we're talking about irrelevant messaging about useless crap. I always marvel at how radio advertising even exists anymore, or at least the way it is practiced. Radio has such a unique advantage over its competitors in that it has the ability to deliver "right time and right place," and yet all this potential is wasted. If I'm driving down Boston Post Road at 12.30 p.m., why wouldn't I be interested in a $5 Footlong from Subway? Instead, I get inundated with a scourge of poorly-targeted direct-response advertising that utilizes defunct and banal calls to action like a toll-free number, which is repeated literally four to five times in the hope that repetition will somehow instill a random sequence of digits in my pea brain and prompt me to pull over immediately in order to order edible floral arrangements for Mother's Day. Think about the incredible points of friction that need to be overcome in the car in order to make the sale, most notably: 1) memory; 2) the phone call; 3) reaching for a

credit card; and 4) safety. Instead, why couldn't Sirius/XM satellite radio develop an r-commerce (r for radio) solution that ties subscribers' credit card details to a computer vision or voice-activated Shazam meets Siri CarPlay interface? If you were following my innovation mash-up, this would require an inclusive collaboration of automotive, media, and financial services as well as tech industries. So why hasn't it happened already? Your guess is as good as mine. In actual fact, Waze is already kind of doing this with their "interstitials" that activate when a car is at a complete stop, with the ability to reroute as a stopover without disrupting the desired destination!

3. **The best of the new.** Well, this is (or should be) fairly obvious. Fish where the fish are. Utilize the same technology that your customers, prospects, partners, and influencers are using. One of my marketing role models, Rishad Tobaccowalla, was once asked, "What's the next big thing?" He shrugged apologetically and said, "Oh, I don't know. Mobile?" The crowd was expecting a revelation akin to Moses revealing the Ten Commandments on Mount Sinai. Instead, they got a flat hand across the face, saying, "Did you not learn your lesson from digital? Your media dollars should follow media consumption!" A couple of years back, I worked with a large CPG company preparing a digital innovation roadmap. I was confused when I looked at their budget, because there wasn't a line item for mobile, even though they described themselves as—get this—a mobile-centric company. This unnamed CPG client had no mobile app; no mobile messaging strategy; was not experimenting with any emerging technology to enhance the shopper experience; and could not fathom a scenario utilizing mobile pay to transact directly with their customers. I could go on....

4. **The worst of the new.** This is what I call TNBT, or TNBT Syndrome. It stands for The Next Big Thing. This is the lost cause of the lost marketer, swayed by whatever the newspaper or trade magazines say is hot right now. They blow whichever way the winds of hype steer them,

and are constantly chasing their own tails. Tactics in search of strategy. Solutions to nonexistent problems. An all-out shit show. Delete!

I can't think of a *better* (and by better I mean worse) example in recent times than when Burger King decided to jump on the voice-activated Alexa or Siri-esque bandwagon. In this case, a television commercial (a.k.a. the worst of the old) that had taken an already low bar (interruptive, irrelevant) and lowered it even further by adding (invasion of privacy) insult to injury. The commercial asked, "Okay, Google, what is the Whopper burger?" In so doing, it prompted any active Google Home device to call up the Wikipedia page for the Whopper. What they expected was, "The Whopper is a burger consisting of a flame-grilled patty made with 100 percent beef with no preservatives or fillers, topped with sliced tomatoes, onions, lettuce, pickles, ketchup, and mayonnaise, served on a sesame-seed bun." What they got back, thanks to the ability to edit Wikipedia entries, was:[2]

"The Whopper is a burger consisting of a flame-grilled patty made with 100% rat and toenail clippings...."

"The 'Whopper' is a cancer-causing hamburger...."

"The 'Whopper' is the worst hamburger product sold by the international fast-food restaurant chain Burger King."

"The Whopper is a burger consisting of a flame-grilled patty made with 100% medium-sized child with no preservatives or fillers, topped with sliced tomatoes, onions, lettuce, cyanide, pickles...."

"[The Whopper] has undergone several reformulations, including resizing and bread changes, yet it remains far inferior to the Big Mac."

Just because you can, doesn't mean you should!

If you see this as a catch-22, you'd be right. Try out new approaches, but be prepared to be ridiculed in the process! You're faced with the reality you're going to make mistakes when it comes to experimentation. I guess that's why they call it an experiment, right? Just don't be dumb. Don't feed an alligator by hand. Don't get too close to fireworks when setting them off. Don't use stupid marketing tactics for the sake of it.

INNOVATIVE. INSANITY. INMATE.

Innovation, by definition, is the act of doing different things to get a different result (and a positive one, at that.) Contrast that with insanity, which was defined by Einstein as doing the same thing over and over again, expecting a different result. There's actually a third category, inspired by a conversation I had with a senior executive who told me that they keep on doing the same thing over and over again and *are resigned to accept* the same result. When you knowingly continue to do something that is harmful to your brand and/ or company and are prepared to accept the same outcome, that is egregious bordering on criminal. Lock them up! Lock them up!

CHAPTER 7

WHAT'S YOUR HERESY?

I WAS AT A CONFERENCE ABOUT 10 YEARS AGO WHEN I HEARD A KEY-note by Andrew Winston.[1] Andrew is the author of *The Big Pivot* and *Green to Gold*. He's an environmentalist, focused on sustainability and how companies navigate mega-challenges. I once heard that a good keynote is one from which you walk away remembering at least one key point. This is even better when it's the exact point the keynote speaker *wanted* you to take away. Sometimes, all people remember from my keynotes are the hashtags like #covfefe or #hashtag!

That day, I walked away intrigued by his concept of embracing your heresy. It inspired me to internalize the information and develop intellectual property around it. This is what we consultants call creative skatting (I made that up, but it sounds credible.)

I could write an entire book on this philosophy, and I almost did. I've even developed entire workshops around embracing your heresy to define your legacy. In this chapter, I'll give you the highlights.

If corporations are to have any chance of staying afloat, they are going to have to ask (and answer) tough questions and deal with the inconvenient truths they fear the most.

THE RESURRECTION OF COMMON SENSE

Marketing is common sense, but how many of us have common sense? Customer service is obvious, but how many of us see the wood for the trees when we're clouded in the day-to-day minutia that destroys creativity? In countless keynotes around the world, I tell my audiences, "I've failed if you all get super excited and motivated, only to return to the office to 1,000 unread emails and a plethora of 'fires' to put out!"

Here's another common sense piece of advice: *do the right thing, even if it is the hardest thing.* Keep that in mind as I attempt to blow your mind with ten ways you can embrace your heresy....

HERESY #1: WHAT IF YOU FIRED YOURSELF?

In 1985, facing the rapid decline of their core business of memory chips, Intel's president, the late Andy Grove, and CEO Gordon Moore fired and then rehired themselves. They did this in response to the question, "If we got kicked out and the Board brought in a new CEO, what do you think s/he would do?" The subsequent answer was, "S/he would get us out of memories." And so they did just that, and began the move from memory chips to microprocessors. And the rest is history.

Why did this symbolic act need to be done at all? Surely, it was a little overdramatic and unnecessary, just to make a point Or maybe it wasn't symbolic at all, but a literal demonstration of what it takes to break the cycle of legacy, incumbency, ingrained thinking, deep-rooted relationships, and biases.

Turning your back on your own company is a heretical act—walking out the door at the expense of your own job security in order to wipe the slate clean and begin again.

HERESY #2: WHAT IF ADVERTISING WENT AWAY?

It's a simple question of heretical proportions: *what if your paid media budget went away? What if you literally had zero paid media? What if advertising went away altogether?*

Think it's a crazy thought? It isn't. You all know the two golden rules of customer service, right? Rule #1: The customer is always right. Rule #2: If the customer is wrong, see rule #1.

So I created my own heretical version:

Axiom #1: Given the choice, 100 times out of 100, consumers would choose to ignore, eliminate, opt out from, or eradicate advertising.

Axiom #2: Advertising is not going away, but remember, when advertising to consumers, see Axiom #1.

I guess the point I was trying to make is that it's better to start off on the back foot, with the assumption that advertising is (a necessary) evil. This way, we have to fight hard and work harder to deliver an acceptable work product.

To be completely honest, I'm not so sure advertising isn't going away. I feel like my earlier statement is playing it somewhat safe; hedging so as to not piss off the media moguls.

We need only look to Brazil as a reminder of what is to come. In 2007, the Municipality of São Paulo introduced its Clean City Law (Lei Cidade Limpa), and over 15,000 billboards went buh-bye. Just like that.

Despite the obvious pot-calling-the-kettle-black irony of describing advertising as ugly amidst the ultimate concrete jungle that is São Paulo, in addition to recent suggestions to begin reintroducing billboards in a very limited fashion, it was nonetheless a shot across the bow that advertising's days were numbered.

Brazil didn't stop there. Election advertising, alcohol and tobacco, elements of medical care, and prostitution carry heavily regulated, partial, or even complete bans.

And forget about a new generation of consumers growing up somewhat tolerant of advertising. Brazil's National Council of the Rights of the Child and the Adolescent (Conselho Nacional dos Direitos da Criança e do Adolescente, or CONANDA) issued Resolution No. 163 on March 13, 2014, banning ads targeting children under the age of 12.

Want a few more proof points? How about Apple's iOS with built-in ad blockers? Or the DVR industry, with automatic skip functions that now fast-forward through an entire advertising pod with one click of the yellow letter "D" on the TiVO remote? At the time I wrote *Life After the 30-Second Spot*, TiVO was still a little on the fence about what their go-to market killer app was. You couldn't skip an entire advertising pod or even a single commercial with the touch of a button; you could only fast-forward commercials. There was, however, a hidden Easter egg where you could convert your fast-forward button into a 30-second skip functionality.

The realization of advertising's heresy is inevitable, and even if it isn't, I believe it's a far smarter and more responsible place to begin. What if it did go away? What if the government charged a tax on it? Why wouldn't advertising become a pariah, just like the tobacco industry? Is it far fetched to see a world in which advertising is regulated up the wazoo?

In practical terms, the way you deal with this heresy is threefold: 1. Assume what you do next year looks *nothing* like what you did last year. 2. Start with a clean slate; the proverbial blank canvas. Wipe your memories and biases clean with a merit-based planning and buying methodology that levels the playing fields between new entrants, challengers, and incumbents. Don't worry; you can still be the godfather of your best client's newborn child. 3. Imagine you literally had zero budget for advertising. What would you do differently? Would this force you to be a little more...dare I say...entrepreneurial?

After factoring in new trends, players, offerings, emerging technology, and platforms, I find it hard to believe you'd end up with a media plan that looks anything like its predecessor.

HERESY #3: WHAT IF YOU GAVE AWAY THE PRODUCT YOU SOLD FOR FREE...AND *STILL* NO ONE WANTED IT?

Allow me to present the newspaper.

A study was done amongst millennials in which they received a daily newspaper for free for a period of two weeks. After this period ended, they were asked if they would pay to receive the newspaper, moving forward. *"Hells, no,"* they replied in unison. Then they were asked what would happen if they were to continue receiving it for free, and their response was a shocking repudiation. In other words, *nope.* When probed as to why they wouldn't want to receive a leading newspaper for free, their responses include environmental (why slaughter innocent trees?) and pragmatic (who wants to receive yesterday's news when you have—you guessed it—the Internet?) And then there was the whole ink-on-the-hands thing.

Another well-known, obvious example is the music industry. For too long, the stalwarts of the music biz held onto their stubborn, arrogant position that their content was so valuable that it had to be purchased in the form of an album (remember those?) Today, the all-you-can eat subscription has replaced à la carte commerce. Pandora and Spotify became the legal successors to the free and illegal Limewire and Napster. And if you needed any reason to give Apple any more money, then add Apple Music to your i-Portfolio.

For music buffs out there and people older than 40, the music industry had its roots in the release of a single on vinyl. The single was on side A, and then there was a "people who like song X might also like song Y" on side B. Two shots at selling an entire album. Then, somehow (greed? cluelessness?), the only way to get the single was by purchasing the album. Earning a customer's dollar moved from being a right to an entitlement. Today, buying albums is dead. Buying singles is dead. Arguably, the music industry is dead.

CROAKED

If only the industry had listened to a frog. A Spiralfrog. Back in 2006, when I launched my first company, crayon, we enjoyed an exciting 6+ months of work on Musicloads (which rebranded as Spiralfrog). The elevator pitch was simple: free AND legal. Free and illegal already existed, but it was infested with viruses, porn bait 'n' switch, and poor-quality tracks. Viruses were a major deterrent, but consumers seemed to tolerate (even enjoy) the porn, and surprisingly, seemed to tolerate less-than-perfect quality.

All Spiralfrog had to do was get all the major players to say "I'm in," and to tolerate one another *en masse* in the ultimate display of "the enemy of my enemy is my friend." So, how did it end for Spiralfrog? Well, let's put it this way: Spiralfrog became frogs' legs.

Corporations just aren't good collaborators. They don't play well in the same sandbox inside their own walls, and even less so outside.

This heresy is so important for the reason the music industry discovered: **your customer's loyalty is not an entitlement.**

HERESY #4: WHAT IF YOU TURNED YOUR BACK ON YOUR CUSTOMER?

My daughter tells me the following joke: *where's the one place you'd be safe during a Zombie Apocalypse? The answer is Costco. They have plenty of food. Plenty of water. And you need a membership card to get in.*

Costco is very clear about whom they want and don't want as their customer. If you're not prepared to spend $60 on a Gold Star Membership (their lowest tier), they'll gladly show you to the door.

The thinking behind the notion that not everyone can be your customer is not necessarily new or revolutionary, though at the time, the concept of "firing your customer" certainly was. In the business-to-business world, there are far too many small and medium-sized businesses, in particular, that endure short-term gain (we need the business and the cash flow) in exchange for long-term pain (running unprofitable accounts; not getting paid on time; having contracts cancelled midstream).

I may be paranoid, but I think American Airlines has got me figured out. I'm pretty sure their Executive Platinum department has me flagged as a high-maintenance customer/complainer. I don't believe I am. I just like things to work (and to go my way every single time.) To be fair, American is getting so much better at customer service in an industry judged by the one that "sucks the least." When I talk to them on Twitter, they know exactly who I am. It wasn't always this way. They do it with little insider quips like "enjoy your window seat." They are "flipping the funnel" by marrying two key databases: their frequent customers and influencers. Not exactly rocket science, but I assure you, not many are doing this. They are also "paying attention" by taking notes on every call and sharing this with one another.

HERESY #5: WHAT IF YOU GOT RID OF THE VERY PRODUCT YOU WERE SELLING?

Okay, this one is a bit of a trip.

Let's get back to my favorite pet project, Barnes & Noble. What if B&N stopped selling books? Absurd? Hardly. Just look at their digital nemesis, Amazon. Even back in the day, when Amazon _was_ in the book business, founder Jeff Bezos would have corrected you if you said Amazon was an online bookseller that happened to provide great customer service. He would have sad, "We're a great customer service company that happens to sell books." Today, I purchase my hair gel there. I purchase my dog's Astroturf pee-pads there. I purchase Nu-Go bars there. I purchase light bulbs there. The only books I purchase are not even real. They're digital books on my Kindle, or audio books via Audible (an Amazon company) on my iPhone.

Barnes & Noble gets literally 0% of my "book" budget.

Let's take a moment of silence to mourn for B&N. In February of 2018, they announced a fresh round of layoffs affecting 1,800 staff. The departures came after a dismal holiday season that saw sinking sales. Are you surprised? Shares in the chain have fallen over 50 percent from a year ago. According to *Fortune*, the bookseller has also seen sales drop for seven straight quarters as of late last year.

Perhaps it's time to rethink their focus, or adjust it if survival is a priority. Consider this: they sell toys (just ask Toys R Us if this is a viable retail business nowadays). They sell vinyl (Gary Dell'Abate from Howard Stern approves, but he's the only one). They sell magazines (see earlier heresy about newspaper). I believe the future of Barnes & Noble lies in real estate. They could cut their physical footprint by half or even more, and not only maintain their revenues and profitability, but even increase them. How? I won't give you one answer. I'll give you five:

1. An all-digital experience, but this would mean sunsetting their Nook (and this might mean getting into bed with a competitor like Apple —see heresy #8.)

2. An experiential playground utilizing VR or interactive billboards that allows consumers to walk into a book and become a part of it, combined with lateral, complementary partnerships. Why not lie back on a tanning bed and listen to the first chapter and when you're ready to purchase, buy from where you left off, or choose an à la carte chapter?

3. We can 3-D print organs, food, guns, and automobiles. So why not books? And to make it a bit more fun, why not customize to your heart's content and choose your font style, color, size, and even paper stock, including biodegradable pages or ones you can plant, a musty retro vintage look and feel that resembles a first edition...or go edible. Hey, it works for condoms.

4. Barnes & Noble has membership that gives pretty awesome discounts on everything in the store. I would take a leaf out of Costco's book and turn a perceived weakness into strength. Not a member? Well, then you can't come into the store. Want that new Omorosa, Scaramucci, or Woodward tell-all book the same day it comes out? Sorry, you'll need to wait two days

for your free shipping from Amazon to kick in. Want to meet for a cup of Joe while your kids play in the kid area? Tough Luck, but please enjoy your cold mochas delivered courtesy of the Amazon drone.

5. I saved the best for last: Sure, B&N could convert their stores into smaller, more productive and profitable ones, but what if they didn't or couldn't because of legacy leases? I would take the unused and underutilized real estate and transform it into a true local, communal hive of activity—a farmer's market. A place where local artisans, creators, and makers could show off their creativity; a new home for antiquing or even tag sales. The possibilities are endless.

HERESY #6: WHAT IF YOU SLAUGHTERED THE CASH COW?

In February of 2007, Netflix shipped their billionth DVD, and then promptly shut it down a few months later to focus on cloud and streaming services, which had been created in October 2006.

It takes a certain kind of bravery or heresy to shun your moneymaker, but when you live a life of heresy, getting out on top is all part of the deal.

The phrase *too good to last* couldn't ring truer in a world in which tomorrow looks nothing like yesterday.

INTERNATIONAL BUSINESS MACHINES: THE GREATEST ESCAPE ARTIST SINCE HARRY HOUDINI

IBM (known then as Big Blue) was a behemoth—a mainframe monolith with a seemingly unassailable stranglehold on the market. After all, before "no one got fired for buying Facebook" or "no one got fired for putting TV on the plan," there was "no one got fired for buying IBM mainframes."

When I came to the United States from South Africa, I worked on the IBM brand business at the Madison Avenue shop Ogilvy & Mather. I was assigned to the small & medium business account. Thanks for nothing! Trying to convince mom-and-pops and medium-sized businesses to purchase PC Servers,

AS/400s, and RS/6000s—what a joke! After all, this was the company ruled by the Trumpesque Lou Gerstner, the man who pulled all his advertising from *Fortune* magazine when they ran an article about him that he didn't like!

IBM doubled down on their dream of transformation. They launched their new tagline, "solutions for a small planet," and embraced their own heresy by shunning the standard operating practice of displaying the product (hardware) in their advertising, replacing their boxes with beautiful glossy photographs of real people, showing off their army of consultants representing their Global Services division. This was a good seven years before Dove's Campaign for Real Beauty gave the middle finger to corrupt beauty norms.

IBM did not stop there.

Today, the company has continued this metamorphosis from a tangible monstrosity to a slick, stealthy, intangible mix of cloud, big data, AI, and iOT.

So, are you ready to turn your back on your core business, and shed the excess weight in favor of a brand-new skin?

HERESY #7: ARE YOU PREPARED TO LEAVE MONEY ON THE TABLE?

Moore's Law is like being on acid. It's mind-blowing and hallucinogenic. If you don't know what Moore's Law is, I hope the following definition will help you: "*Moore's law is the observation that the number of transistors in a dense integrated circuit doubles approximately every two years.*"

Actually, I'm not sure that helped me.

In layman's terms, it means there is a disproportionate relationship between tech power and the cost to produce that power!

To prove the point: the iPhone 5S was released in September 2013. Had it been produced in 1991, it would have cost $3.56 million to manufacture a single unit: the processer, memory, and communication speed (not including the camera, operating system, display, apps, and motion detectors!)

Moore's Law was designed to separate the heretics from the greedy denizens on borrowed time. Here are two examples:

Before AT&T's $10/day for international roaming, data was really expensive when traveling abroad. Back in the day (like two years ago), I would pay something like $60 for 120 MB of "international" data over a 30-day period (#highwayrobbery). Then, one day, I called to complain, and the customer service representative asked me why I wasn't paying $30 for 120 MB. For the same amount ($60), I could get more than double the data (300MB).

I said, *"Uh, does Chuck Norris know Victoria's Secret?"* Obviously.

And then I asked, *"I'm just curious...how long have you had this new pricing policy in place?"*

The response: six months.

I lost it.

"Why didn't you tell me?"

"Well, we can't exactly tell every one of our customers every time we change any of our pricing programs. How would we do that?"

"Well sure you can," I said. *"Just send us a !#!%$%#$#& text message!"*

Contrast this with Apple, who sent me the following note (ironically, when I was traveling to the U.K.):

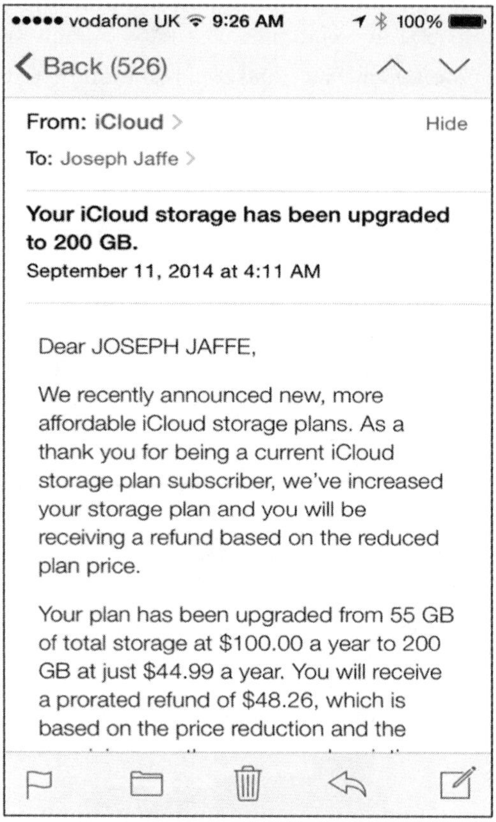

Figure 7.1 - Leaving Money on the Table

Not only did they proactively upgrade me to the better offering, they prorated the cost savings and refunded me.

To you, this might seem like heresy. To me, it's common decency. Or just common sense. Or just good business sense.

Want one more example? How about when outdoor and active lifestyle retailer REI closed all their stores on Black Friday? The message? Simple: get outside (and use your products, of course, to maximize the experience!) Smart idea? Well, consider the fact that Cyber Monday (or more likely Cyber Week) eclipsed Black Friday sales in 2018 for the first time in history!

Leaving money on the table in the short term is sure to reap rewards in the longer term. This is radical transparency at its finest and most heretical.

HERESY #8: ARE YOU PREPARED TO FUND YOUR COMPETITOR?

Who is your real competitor? Do they even exist today? In the startup world, there is no such thing as a non-disclosure agreement (NDA), or at least good luck getting a venture capitalist (VC) to sign one. The truth is, as great an idea as you think yours is, there are probably three to five entrepreneurs doing the exact same thing as you are right this very second, AND they're probably further along than you are.

The startup world recognizes that life is too short to be paranoid and neurotic, or to keep one's cards too close to the chest. In other words, just like a large company. Sometimes, the move to embrace your competitor and even collaborate with them can lead to surprising outcomes.

This happened when Apple opened up their walled garden to arch-rival Microsoft, when they allowed their iPod OS to be compatible with Microsoft Windows/PCs. Whether this move was magnanimous, desperate, calculated, or compromised is irrelevant. In my opinion, it singlehandedly saved Apple, or at least propelled them to the eminent status they hold today. The popularity and growth of the iPod was the growth catalyst or tipping point that saw Apple rebound to become the world's first trillion-dollar company.[1]

By inviting the Windows Operating System to the party, they also created a pretty significant counteraction: the acceleration of the demise of the abominable Zune. Apple actually did Microsoft a favor, sparing countless millions from subsequently investing in this white elephant. In other words, a win-win outcome occurred that would have never happened without a heresy "play," or perhaps I should say "fast-forward."

Another example is Mixify, a 2015 collaboration between Pepsi, Coca-Cola, and Keurig Dr. Pepper. Apparently, the only thing worse than competition is obesity, which is why these nemeses teamed up to beg us to get off our fat asses, and exercise more in order to drink their carbonated sugar water products in moderation.

How long did this collaboration last? How much staying power or endurance did these heretics have? To answer that question, just visit mymixify.com, the initiative's official website...

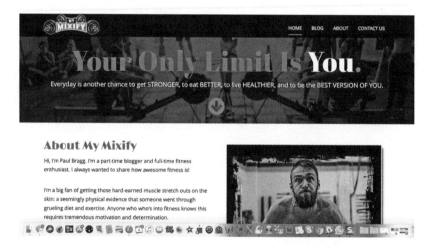

Figure 7.2 - Never Let Your URL's Expire

HERESY #9: WHAT IF YOU PUT YOURSELF OUT OF BUSINESS?

It's 2025, and your company files for bankruptcy. How did it happen?

It's a heretical position to question your right to exist, but it's a necessary one. I'm not sure why corporate existentialism is not the perfect corporate colonic. What if 100 years of history were NOT an asset, but in fact a liability? Rather than celebrate your company's centenary, perhaps you should throw a premature wake?

When I pose the question, "Can <u>anyone</u> in this room say with certainty that you'll be around in another 50 years' time? How about five years' time?" I have yet to see one executive put their money where their mouth is. If you believe you are bulletproof or future-proof, prove it. And if you think you're the exact opposite, what are you doing about it?

In a practical sense, the way to institutionalize this kind of thinking is to eliminate business as usual and "the way it's always been done." Welcome new ideas and challenges to existing norms, standards, and practices. Welcome them from everyone, and everywhere. Clearly, in order to do so, you'll need to deal head on with those who would vehemently oppose this approach—the ones with the most to lose by changing.

You can do this the hard way (be prepared to unlearn your bad habits and go back to "school" to acquire new skills) or the harder way (hit the road, bones). For those willing to try, I do think there is a way to soften the blow and reduce the perceived risk, especially if compensation, job security, or "tenure" is involved.

> "A culture that allows people to fail is a culture that opens itself up to the possibility that they will not only succeed, but succeed gloriously."

That's all well and good, but this isn't a game. Nor is it a training program. This is war. And you're being attacked at every imaginable flank and on every possible front. Whether from the incumbents, rising stars, or the next wave of graduates from the backyard shed, winter is coming!

So why wait for the White Walkers to come to your doorstep? Take the battle to them! If someone is going to put you out of business, shouldn't it be you?

If only the magazine industry had embraced this particular heresy during the early days of the Internet. I remember being hired by Condé Nast to go down to Jamaica circa 2004 to speak at a *Modern Bride/Brides* offsite on the topic of digital disruption. I guess my brief was, "Don't pull any punches. Tell us about how the world is changing...but you should be mindful and wary of the litany of sensitivities, political minefields, insecurities, and personalities and egos in the room." Riiiiiiight.

I get this a lot: *be honest, but not too honest.* So naturally, I told them the truth: "I want you to think of your dot-com property on an equal footing or billing as your print publication." That was it! I might as well have taken a knee during the national anthem in a stadium filled with Confederate-statue-loving patriots! I could literally see the daggers thrusting out of the publisher's eyes in my general direction. It was a lonely night on the beach.

Thankfully, the check cleared.

Of course, I was right. *Modern Bride* closed down in 2009. And in August of 2018, Robert A. Sauerberg, Jr., Chief Executive of Condé Nast, announced that the company would be selling off—you guessed it—*Brides* magazine. Guess the brainiacs at Boston Consulting Group who helped Sauerberg come up with this recommendation envisioned a future in which people didn't get married anymore. On the upside, that would also mean less divorce, so there's that....

Breathe a sigh of relief, and be thankful you don't work in the magazine business. Unless you do—in which case, don't worry; be happy. You can always move to Colorado. In all seriousness, please hear me clearly when I tell you that whether you work in the magazine business or not, there isn't a single business or industry that won't be affected in the most profound ways.

Take the plastic funny money business (also known as credit cards), for example. In a cashless, contactless, plastic-less world, who holds the keys to the future? American Express? Visa? Or the likes of PayPal and their adopted child, Venmo?

The restroom at the Independence Beer Garden next to Philadelphia's Liberty Bell is in some kind of mobile trailer. Go there and you'll meet Lyndell Westbrook, a restroom attendant who hands you your towels and soap, and, of course, the usual *accoutrements* like breath mints, cologne, candy, and the like.

He also accepts Venmo!

Venmo is proof positive that you don't need to get your hands dirty when transacting, and nowhere is this more prevalent than in a bathroom! So, let's try an experiment. I'd like you to send a minimum of $1 to @A1Bathroom via Venmo.

Figure 7.3 - @A1Bathroom on Venmo

Let's make him a millionaire! He deserves it. He is a natural innovator, and he's helping you become one, too.

Actually, let's try another experiment: include me, as well. I'm @jaffejuice on Venmo. Just $1 will get you a shout-out on Twitter. Let me know what you'd like me to say in the comments. And if you really want to supersize this, send me *whatever* you believe this book is worth in terms of value delivered to you. Perhaps you'll want to book me directly using Venmo as your offer? As a benchmark, I once got diamonds sent to me in appreciation of a measurable lift of $2,000,000 on a company's bottom line thanks to the ideas from Flip the Funnel....so, anything is possible, right?

I'll track everything and share the results of both experiments with you via www.builttosuck.com under bonus content.

It's not hard to cannibalize your own business. You actually can't lose. After all, if it fails, then it's business as usual. If it succeeds so wildly that it puts you out of business, you now have a new starlet and successor to the throne. This is evolution and heresy marketing at its core—and at its best! Survival of the fittest.

HERESY #10: WHAT IF YOU COULD DO A HARD RESET?

Imagine walking away from it all. Your 100+ years of history. Your plaques, awards, and oil paintings of your white male founders. Your secret formulas. Your dirty secrets. Your brand guidelines. Your union contracts. Your biases. Your baggage.

Go to Google and type in the word *McDonald's*, then click on IMAGES. You'll see a sanitized version of utopia, thanks to a combination of terrific content marketing and search-engine optimization. Give those agencies a raise!

Dig a little deeper and type in a question like *is McDonald's good for you*, and you'll get a whole different set of responses. Quick—withdraw that bonus from said agencies.

So, is the problem here that a content specialist dropped the ball and didn't do their propaganda—er, due diligence—a little more thoroughly? Not at all. The real issue is simply that McDonald's is a major contributor towards obesity—specifically childhood obesity.

Isn't it time for McDonald's to acknowledge their role in the sobering reality that fast food is the devil? The argument *guns don't kill people...the people who pull the trigger do* might work for the NRA (though latest financials[1] do not paint an overly rosy picture for the "good guys"), but does the same argument apply to the quick-service restaurant business?

What if McDonald's had a scale at every outlet? What if you had to step on that scale on your way to the cash register? What if the scale set off on alarm if you were over 300 pounds? What if the McDonald's dollar menu was tied to your body mass index (BMI), and the only way to pay a buck was to be in shape? What if McDonald's refused to serve you if your BMI was in the danger zone? What if the federal government stepped in and regulated this...or even mandated it?

Once again, if you think this is all crazy talk, you'd be wrong:

- Every fast-food chain with more than 20 outlets must, by law, list the calories in every food item on the menu. Sure, some patrons will ignore this, but others will be shocked and nauseated at the fact that your typical large order of French fries in pretty much any fast food outlet is close to—or in excess of—1,000 calories.
- Soda machines are already illegal in schools.
- Ex-NYC Mayor Michael Bloomberg attempted to outlaw the Big Gulp.

And how long before it becomes illegal to poison consumers with additives, preservatives, and other ingredients that sound more like a science experiment than something edible?

So, what should McDonald's do about it? The answer is to get out in front of the problem: be proactive and provocative, dare to care, and take extreme steps to be at the forefront of change.

So what if McDonald's created (or acquired) the Fitbit, or a similar accelerometer-powered wristband? A calorie-counting LED screen that visualized your daily calorie-burning goal in the shape of a Big Mac and offered a simple congratulatory message upon hitting your goal, like, "You've earned your Big Mac, bud!" May sound trite, but it's a start....

Ironically, and like so many corporate slumbering giants, McD's came to the party with too little, too late: an inept kiddie fitness band that was part of the children's Happy Meal. Adding insult to injury, it was cheaply manufactured somewhere offshore, and ended up giving kids skin rashes.

Not surprisingly, it was promptly withdrawn and discontinued.

This doesn't mean it wasn't a good idea; just extremely poorly executed as a nice-to-have tactic versus a strategic business imperative.

Heresy marketing is perhaps the ONLY way for corporations to suck less, and in doing so, to embrace the very change that would otherwise fell them and render them obsolete.

It's the only solution right now for dealing with the massive defection of talent in favor of the startup tsunami fast approaching.

CHAPTER 8

WHAT'S YOUR LEGACY?

WHEREVER I GO IN THE WORLD, I TEND TO GET ASKED THE SAME questions over and over again. I used to get asked one recurring question in the Q&A, until I put it in every one of keynotes as an upfront slide: *"Joe, what's the next big thing?"* To which I always respond, *"There is no next big thing, you moron...the next big thing is NOW!"* I'll expand on that particular question later, but of late, I now have a new "worst" question: *"Hey Joe, who's doing it right?"*

I hate this question for the following reasons:

1. Why are you so concerned about everyone else?

2. Why are you not focusing on being the best possible version of yourselves and sticking to core business fundamentals and principles, like treating customers right? A golfer focuses on his or her individual game. Plays each shot as if it is the only one. Occasionally hears a roar from the crowd, but shuts it out and doesn't get distracted.

3. Every company and every industry is different. Why do you believe their triumphs and tragedies will translate and apply perfectly to your business?

4. Why does it matter? If I tell you to be more like Nike, will you? Can you?

Instead, perhaps I should share a list of all the companies who are doing it wrong. How much time do you have?!

A cursory look at Glassdoor's annual "Best Places to Work" list reveals companies like Lululemon, Google, Nike, Starbucks, and Apple. It is not a coincidence that the companies I write about glowingly in this book feature in the list, whereas companies I am more critical of do not....

With that said, I would caution you to avoid comparisons. Instead of sucking less than *the other guy*, your mission in life should be *to suck the least*. Or better yet, not to suck at all. Period. This reminds me of a blog post I wrote back in 2007 on Jaffe Juice:

> It's unbelievable to me how many industries fall into the universal suckage category. Case in point, the wireless/cellular category. Cingular (part of the new AT&T) bills itself as the network with the "lowest amount of dropped calls." *In other words, choose us because we suck the least!* The airline industry talks about the most on-time arrivals or departures.
>
> Here's a thought: how about not dropping any calls or arriving and departing on time ALL THE TIME.
>
> Corporations fall into a death trap of believing that consumers don't really have choice when it comes to a subset of providers who all subscribe to the same low bar of service and/or expectations. This might be true in the short term, but it also lays the table for a hungry, aggressive, intense, and innovative challenger brand to wreak havoc on the incumbents.

Let's get back to our golf game. Apparently, you're stuck with me as your caddy. As I just mentioned, the pros play an individual game, even if they're paired in a trio or quartet. Sometimes, it's pretty intimidating when you have a Tiger in the tank. The pros will tell you this doesn't affect them. They just play their normal game, taking every shot as it comes. When they force a shot or try and play to the crowd, things typically go pear-shaped.

They receive advice from a caddy (me), who carries a playbook of sorts with yardages and recommended clubs. Well, this book is your playbook. Keep your own score, but don't look at the overall scoreboard until perhaps the 18th and final hole—and even then, it's really there for the spectators. In the same spirit of the occasional roar from the crowd signifying a looooooooong birdie putt, a brilliant bunker recover landing inches from the pin, and in extremely rare instances, the elusive hole-in-one, I'll give you a few highlights from "around the course" (*companies doing it well*), but in general, I'll tell you to keep your head down, follow through, and Stay. The. Course.

So, my response to "who's doing it right?" is **NOBODY**. Seriously, amongst large, public companies that are built to suck, no one is killing it, and if you think they are, that's just called good P.R.!

Even I fall into the trap sometimes. In this book, I talk pretty effusively about IBM, but for every gold star, there is an equal and opposite demerit—from the earlier reference to aspiring oncologist, Dr. Watson, to the fact that IBM-registered[1] 22 straight quarters of declining revenues, as reported in January 2018. This number is almost back to where they were 20 years ago (not coincidentally, when I stopped working on their business). Attempting to stay relevant comes with a price. According to employee insiders, it has become an aggressively exploitative environment for their employees and contractors.

Most companies are a fragile house of cards. When I talk to people inside these companies about some of the accolades they receive in the press and trades, they roll their eyes and scoff at the disconnect between the perception from the outside and the reality of the dysfunction internally.

If you only knew the truth....

The Lean Startup movement has become a cult of sorts. It was hailed as the messiah for corporations looking to undertake a metamorphosis into a leaner, more agile self. G.E. became the poster child for this new approach—a case study in how a behemoth company could, in fact, buck the trend to suck. At the time, Beth Comstock was their global chief marketing officer. She was extremely visible, public, and a master of earned media. Are you surprised that she has since left the company to focus on her own "personal brand?"

Jeff Gothelf, author of *Sense & Respond* and *Lean vs. Agile vs. Design Thinking*, wrote an article which I believe captures the hopelessness of corporations—and pinning any kind of hope on them to show us the way out of this mess. You can read the full article at www.builttosuck.com under the bonus content tab, but here is a small excerpt:

> Crisis demands a scapegoat and many were quick to blame long-time CEO Jeff Immelt's firm belief in Lean Startup as the cause for his and the stock price's demise. If it wasn't directly responsible, then at the very least Lean Startup served as a distraction away from GE's core competencies, the critics said. Lean Startup is not the cause of poor financial results. If anything, it's a magnifying glass that reveals antiquated planning practices not suitable for a software-driven world.

SO, WHO'S DOING IT WRONG?

Well, if it's true that no one is doing it right, then the corollary that everyone is doing it wrong has to apply.

According to Coresight Research, 7,066 U.S. retail stores closed in 2017. As an aside, there were also 3,157 announced store openings. The fact that Dollar General and Dollar Tree accounted for 62 percent says something, for sure.

That number is only going up. Using a different metric, according to the CoStar Group, 2017 saw 105 million square feet of retail space disappear. By the end of the second quarter in 2018, this number was already at 94 million square feet.

In the U.S., the fourth Friday in November is endearingly known as Black Friday. It is the biggest shopping day of the year, and is historically the day that retail stores go into "the black." It is also the day after Thanksgiving, and these days, no one is more thankful than the surviving retailers who draw on this day as one final Hail Mary play.

Unfortunately for them, said retailers are more likely to be left black and blue than reveling in greenbacks. According to eMarketer, Amazon will take home almost 50 percent of all e-commerce spent in the U.S. in 2018 (49 cents on every dollar spent, compared to 44 cents the year before).

Holy shit!

If you buy into the fact companies like Sears are just operating on borrowed time, not even an earlier foray into e-commerce could have turned this unfolding horror story around.

The Titanic did not spot the deadly iceberg until it was too late. It could not alter course, reverse direction, or avoid a head-on collision. Instead, the focus shifted wholly to minimizing loss (death). Folks, this is where we are right now. Your best-case scenario is all about making the best of a bad situation. In a sense, you are living your heresy right now.

Your professional hell is self-inflicted due to an obsession with acquisition, reliance on tactics, and an absolute aversion to risk. Your distraction has diverted your attention from what you should have been doing: investing in a series of well-timed, well-structured, well-calculated bets on the future, mixed in with deep seated commitment to continuous change.

Don't try to eliminate, mitigate, or manage risk. Instead, embrace it. When things feel too comfortable, too calm, and too quiet, it is not the beginning of the end; it is the end.

~~WHAT'S~~ WHEN'S YOUR SEARS MOMENT?

Every single industry will soon enough (if it hasn't happened already) come face to face with its own mortality. Instead of lamenting how it came to this, why not embrace the idea that you were always operating on borrowed time?

When things were going right, you gladly took the credit for how you taught the world to sing in perfect harmony, when the only *real thing* was your gift of type-2 diabetes to the world. But now that things are turning sour, you're feverishly updating your resume and gleefully planning for your next glorious chapter. What was that saying about rats and a sinking ship...?

LET'S PLAY A GAME

Can you identify a single industry that hasn't been (or won't be) affected by the cruel sands of time, the curse of incumbency, and the disease of marketing myopia? Can you show a single company that has made it this far completely untouched, unharmed, and unscathed?

Even the new starlets aren't without their pains—growing or otherwise. Take Uber, for example. The company has outlasted countless scandals, including misogyny, suspect labor practices, and literally paying off hackers following a security breach of its user base and profile information of unprecedented proportions, as well as facing off with major metropolitan centers like London with respect to renewing its contract.

No company is immune to disruption. Disruption does not discriminate. It hates everyone equally.

> "No company is immune to disruption. Disruption does not discriminate. It hates everyone equally."

I want to stress that I am, in fact, a happy, positive, and optimistic person. I believe every person is naturally capable of doing incredible acts of benevolence, generosity, and goodwill. The corporation, however, seems less able to achieve this.

I am reminded of a *Monty Python* skit (though it could have been *Benny Hill*—either way, it was British) in which an Army sergeant says to his troops, "I need a volunteer for a suicide mission." They all step backward except for one poor loser. You, my friend, are he. Good luck in your hopeless cause, but also—don't give up.

Don't wait for someone else to make the first move, either inside your company or outside. Do it yourself, and do it now. Just do it.

What follows is a blueprint that I believe offers you the best chance of survival. Do one of these exceptionally well (as in best-in-class), and you raise your chances of survival. Do two or more, and you make the exponential leap from survival to "thrival," and maybe—just maybe—you'll be (re)built to last.

Today, we prostrate ourselves before the magnificence of WeWork, the shared workspace that has literally become one of the world's most valuable companies.

WeWork is not necessarily a new idea. Actually, it's not a new idea at all. Corporate players like Regus played the rent-an-office game long before WeWork came along. In fact, WeWork wasn't even the first shared/co-working space to tap into the entrepreneurial revolution. First-mover advantage is important, but clearly, in this case, it was more about being best versus being first.

Early 2019, WeWork rebranded itself as The We Company, which recognized the reality this was always a real estate play. After all, CEO Adam Neumann was also his company's biggest landlord! Moving forward, the company will have three main business units: WeWork (office), WeLive (residential) and WeGrow (education).

Figure 8.1 - Rise and Fall of Civilizations

No company lasts forever. Not Apple (Steve Jobs helped bring them back from the brink). Not Facebook. Not Tesla (who laid off 7% of their workforce in early 2019). Not even the We Company.

I was in my daughter's classroom a couple years back, and saw this chart on the wall. It documented 5,000 years of history—specifically, the history of civilizations. It was even neatly color-coded and organized by continent. What you should take away from this is plain and simple.

Nothing lasts forever. Not the Roman Empire. Not the Byzantine Empire. Not the Ottoman Empire. Not the Corporate Empire.

Take Harley-Davidson, for example. I don't think there is a single MBA program out there that doesn't put this "success story" on a pedestal as a best-in-class example of corporate, business, marketing, and brand strategy at its finest. The only problem is that Harley is sucking big time at the moment. With a 40 percent drop in its third-quarter 2017 profit, compared to the same period a year earlier; and, more recently, a 13 percent plunge in U.S. sales in Q3 of 2018—Harley's biggest sales slump in eight years—this icon has been plagued with a new business reality that includes dealing with trade wars, a demographic catch-22 of baby boomers aging out, and younger consumers turning away from hogs and other swines. Vaughn L. Beals, Jr., architect of Harley's famous turnaround in the 80s, died in 2018 at the age of 90. I hope he requested a plot next to that of his beloved brand.

No one is safe! This is the strongest starting point for anyone reading this book. From startup founder to Fortune 500 chairman of the board, infusing a daily mix of humility, paranoia, and self-effacing brutal honesty into your attitude and approach to business is a healthy (and even vital) approach. When every day is a fresh fight for your right to survive, who knows...you just might succeed.

Speaking of which, I also think it's worth thinking about the American empire. My naturalized country, 'Murica, is often referred to (by Americans) as the greatest country in the world. USA! USA! USA! The same country where roughly 50 percent of the voting public believes global warming is a hoax, clean coal is what happens when you give dirty coal a bubble bath, Mandarin is a type of orange, and STEM is a leaf.

Or perhaps we should draw on Will McAvoy's words from the pilot of HBO's *The Newsroom* (2012): *"...there's absolutely no evidence to support the statement that we're the greatest country in the world. We're 7th in literacy, 27th in math, 22nd in science, 49th in life expectancy, 178th in infant mortality, 3rd in median household income, number 4 in labor force, and number 4 in exports. We lead the world in only three categories: number of incarcerated citizens per capita, number of adults who believe angels are real, and defense spending, where we spend more than the next 26 countries combined, 25 of whom are allies."*

I used to scoff at people who call America the greatest country in the world. That is, until I became a citizen and realized we **are** the greatest country in the world!

In complete seriousness, if the United States is to remain dominant—or, at the very minimum, competitive on the global scale and stage—it, too, will have to evolve, face its heresy (which just might be racism), and create a culture of constant disruption and innovation. Then, and only then, it might just beat the odds.

If there is one personality trait that is essential for the journey to survival, it is humility. A talented, open-minded, agile founder with a mediocre idea is always preferable to a stubborn, arrogant, and close-minded entrepreneur with a brilliant one.

If you're in the corporate world, you simply have to discard the superiority complex associated with your grandeur, self-importance, and invulnerability. Take a leaf (or is it STEM?) out of the entrepreneurial playbook and embrace your own fragility, imperfections, and mortality. Your ability to imagine your demise will help give birth to your salvation.

> "Your ability to imagine your demise will help give birth to your salvation."

THE MODEL. FINALLY!

There's foreplay, and then there's four-score-and-seven play. This sits somewhere in the middle.

Pay attention, now.

The recipe for success has four courses, or pillars, and you've signed up for the *prix fixe*. The next four chapters will introduce and expand upon these pillars, setting the table for what hopefully can become your journey to survival.

There are very few companies right now doing more than one of the four pillars really well. So, why shouldn't it be you? Why couldn't it be you?

The world doesn't need another digital marketing book. Or one that focuses on employee engagement. Not another customer service missive. Or one that covers social responsibility.

And that's not what you're going to be getting, either. I hope to bring you unique and fresh takes on each category, infused with an evolved vision that is bold, provocative, and innovative.

After each section, I want you to evaluate what you've gained by asking yourselves these questions:

1. Why are we not doing better at implementing the table stakes "price of entry" elements?

2. For every idea that appears to be "common sense," why is this in short supply within our own company?

3. Don't worry about what the external world is saying about the flavor of the month. What's hot? What's not? Instead of worrying about the next big thing, perhaps we should be asking, *is it the next big thing FOR US?* Too often, we poo-poo something as passé because it appears that the crowd has moved on to the next "big thing." I'm stopping short of saying that Q.R. codes hold the key to your salvation, but I'm also not saying they don't.

Figure 8.2 - Scan this QR code

111

4. What happens when we mix, match, or combine two or more seemingly independent ideas? For example, bringing digital disruption to customer obsession?

5. Instead of playing catch-up or contributing the bare minimum, why wouldn't we throw all caution to the wind and go all in?

SHOW ME THE SURVIVAL

I'll give you examples of companies that are either doing it right or trying their best. With that said, it's a lot easier and more entertaining to call out those who are losing by example. I'll do my best to hate the game versus the playa. The only entity that deserves to be ridiculed and humiliated is an inanimate one: the corporation.

SECTION 3:

DREAMSTATE

CHAPTER 9

DIGITAL DISRUPTION

I called the first pillar *digital disruption* as opposed to *digital innovation* for a few well thought-out reasons:

I have a love-hate relationship with the word *innovation*; mainly because I love it, and most people hate it. For some reason, the corporate bigwigs feel it is overused and clichéd. The irony is palpable, as they are the same hotshots who are the least "innovative." If the best defense is offense, they've taken aim at change in order to preserve the status quo.

Digital is inherently innovative because it incorporates so many game-changing practices, starting with interactive, online, e-commerce, and Web 1.0. Its influence, ownership, and scope doesn't stop there, but go on to encompass everything from Web 2.0 and social media to mobile to the ever-expanding horizon of emerging platforms—including, but not limited to, iOT (Internet of Things), AR/VR/MR (augmented, virtual, and mixed reality), AI (artificial intelligence), computer vision, and blockchain or whatever buzzword your chairman just read in *The Wall Street Journal* and asked you what your "POV" was (and you subsequently asked your agency.)

Disruption has no emotion. It is, in a sense, the beast mode of survival.

At the end of the day, it doesn't matter what we call it. What matters is what we do about it—and by *it*, I refer to being disruptive with a singular purpose: the obliteration of all competitors.

This is the lens I would urge you to apply when thinking about (or rethinking) the role of digital in your organizations. It needs to provide an unfair advantage: a leg up in the survival stakes.

In the corporate world, some might refer to this as *competitive advantage*.

It can be expressed in terms of barriers to entry (for your competitors) or barriers to exit (for your customers). It is deadly like quicksand, and sticky like honey.

COMPETITIVE ADVANTAGE IS, BY DEFINITION, DISRUPTIVE

Years ago, a piece of research caught my eye. It was, if memory serves correctly, conducted by the executive recruitment firm Spencer Stuart, and looked to gauge the priorities of the C-Suite. According to the report, the CEO's top three included: growth, customer intimacy, and competitive advantage.

I translated the CEO hit list into more familiar startup terminology:

Growth = better, cheaper, faster

Customer intimacy = service or "utility"

Competitive advantage = disruption

If it weren't obvious enough, the ultimate goal cannot be survival as an end unto itself. Prolonging inevitable death, or a stay of execution, if you will, is a miserable existence. The journey to survival is a continuous and never-ending one—a means to an end. The real goal is *thrival:* from survival to *thrival.* It is, in other words, growth—or, more accurately in the case of the corporation, a return to growth. Organic growth. Real growth. Customer-driven, authentic growth.

Not purchased growth through M&A Activity. Not fake growth via private equity. Earned growth.

BETTER, CHEAPER, FASTER...PICK TWO

In a world of continuous cost-cutting, budgets are typically shrinking instead of growing; and, for this reason, getting "more from less" has become the norm. This is the life of the corporation. It's a miserable existence when every year, your equity is continuously chiseled away—eroded by the sands of time and the decree of the bean counters.

This is your life. Deal with it.

This is where I believe rapid prototyping and active experimentation can play a key role. Establishing first-mover advantage is a terrific tonic to invigorate tired systems and processes. It's also a direct path to scaling with success: leapfrogging the tired "test 'n' learn toe-dip with a rinse-and-repeat (when things work) or pivot (when things don't) and continuous improvement protocol.

Action: Conduct sufficient experiments that conform to the better, cheaper, faster protocol.

UTILITY AS A PUBLIC SERVICE

Customer intimacy is a much better term than *customer service* or even *customer experience*. The ability to establish, nurture, and grow an authentic relationship with one's customer based upon trust, loyalty, honesty, and mutual respect is a stepping stone toward both growth and competitive advantage.

Economists define functional benefit as the ability to create or add tangible value. Instead of service or experience, why not consider this notion of utility—one that can be expressed or measured in meaningful terms, and one that customers cannot live without?

In this category, one-off campaigns are replaced with initiatives that endure beyond a temporary window. If the better, cheaper, faster category is characterized as a *what* (establishing proof of concept or some kind of positive indicator with promise and potential), then the utility category is the *how*.

Action: Establish multi-month (but not indefinite) partnerships with a curated shortlist or subset of the "better, cheaper, faster" cohort. The goal is to help both sides get to the next level: whether hitting specific goals or milestones (for the startup) or key business, brand health, or customer KPIs (for the corporation).

CHANGE THE GAME OR GO HOME

The only time an incremental step led to an exponential result was when Neil Armstrong implanted his lunar Yeezy on the surface of the moon (or studio, if you believe the conspiracy theories from nuts like Alex Jones.)

Instead, what may be required is a giant leap—possibly a leap of faith, but not necessarily, if there is some kind of process or commitment already in place.

To willingly self-inflict a disruption-sized wound is not the action of a crazed sadist, but rather that of a sober realist; a grounded pragmatist; a visionary optimist.

Action: You can't rent competitive advantage. You need to own it. Companies must think of themselves as investors or even venture capitalists if they are to establish a foothold on the future. In order to secure this kind of dominance, all competitors need to be locked out of the game.

Connect the dots, dummy. Technology holds the key.

DO YOU NEED A SECOND OPINION?

Of course you do.

The consulting firm KPMG published their U.S. CEO 2017 outlook in a report entitled "Disrupt and Grow" (or maybe it should have read "Disrupt TO Grow").

Seventy-two percent of respondents said that "rather than waiting to be disrupted by competitors, their organizations (were) actively disrupting their own sectors;" and yet, "two-thirds of CEOs were concerned their organizations were not disrupting business models in their industry." Sounds like a classic case of one hand not knowing what the other is doing.

What struck me were their top five strategic priorities across the next three years:

1. Greater speed to market (25 percent)

2. **Digitization** of the business (22 percent)

3. Becoming more data-driven (21 percent)

4. Building public trust (21 percent)

5. Implementing **disruptive** technology (20 percent)

I'll go with the daily double combination of line items two and five, and take digital disruption for a billion dollars, Trebek!

Looks like we're on the right track here...or are we?

IT'S NOT INSIDE

My strong contention is that this cannot happen within the walls of your corporation. You truly need to think outside the box. Literally. This isn't something you can do yourself. You can certainly try, but you WILL fail. If this isn't your core business, it probably never will be. When you go it alone, you are taking a ride without a seatbelt on the corporate hype curve.

Almost always, companies must come to the realization that what is required is an external partnership with a best-in-class specialist. Most find out the hard way by getting burned from doing it themselves. The arrogant approach often leads to a period of time on the sidelines, licking their wounds, before the decision is taken to find an outside specialist.

The reality is that digital disruption—and more importantly, the ability to bring them to life—is not coming from inside your company, which is not to say they are not there at all. Employees who do have bold ideas are just not sharing them with you. They are stealthily working on them on the side. Nights and weekends, if you like.

Soon, I'll tell you how you can avoid having this happen to *your* organization, but for now, recognize that the external marketplace is teeming with real businesses with real traction. Don't assume they're waiting for you. More likely, they are lying in wait for you. Don't wait for them to come to you. If anything, they're coming FOR you! Go to them. Find them. Acquire them before they acquire you.

YOU CAN'T BEAT 'EM, SO JOIN 'EM

You had better figure out a way to build a bridge between Madison Avenue (home of the brand) and Mountain View (home of the tech company).

Startups and the entrepreneurs who run them are the epitome of life. They are motivated by very different factors than you are. It's not always money. Often, it's the will to take you down—or even out. They think differently. They act differently. They are hotwired to cut through corporate bullshit like a knife through butter. If *any* of this can rub off on your people and your culture, it's time and money well spent.

But how? This is the tricky part. The default corporate approach is to begin with a test 'n' learn pilot program. A small fraction of these will upgrade to some kind of strategic partnership (often called acceleration), and a microscopic sub-segment will graduate to some kind of investment, or even acquisition. I've worked with countless blue chip companies and executed over 200 individual pilot programs on their behalf. Here are some of my learnings and key takeaways:

1. **Collaboration needs to be a true partnership**. Corporates that drag their feet will ultimately put startups out of business. Startups that see a corporation as a "sugar daddy" will end up souring the relationship by asking for too much, too soon.

2. **Managing expectations is key**. Defining success and measuring success is critical. Work with a startup or new technology platform is ongoing. Goal posts are constantly shifting, and as such, digital disruption must become a mainstay.

3. **There are term limits to mediocrity**. When I worked on the Futures program, we used a cap of 90 days as a viability term associated with getting the pilot to market. If the brand in question could not get their act together within this time, they lost the pilot. This was a valuable lesson at a low cost of entry. Next time, they needed to move faster!

4. **Blue oceans are awesome. Just don't boil them**. Think big. Think bold. Stretch yourselves out of your comfort zone, but at the same time, be realistic in terms of being able to solve billion-dollar-industry or million-dollar-corporate problems with a token honorarium. What you are looking for is what I call proof of life—a sign, a semblance, a crumb of potential to indicate you're on the right track.

5. **Failure is relative. Death is absolute**. The potential for growth and ultimate success is dependent upon allowing for the possibility of failure along the way. More on this shortly.

6. **Stay the course.** Define what success looks like up front, but make sure the very highest person in the pecking order signs off on this. Corporate executives have very short memories. I have seen, time and time again, how short-term enthusiasm reverts to chronic myopia and the familiar refrain, "But how many widgets did we sell?"

7. **Sign a commitment contract.** Force the executives who got so excited at the beginning to follow through with their investment(s). If they make a commitment, they need to see it through.

8. **Rewrite the rules.** Tear up your onerous master service agreements, terms and conditions, scope-of-work templates, insurance requirements, and lengthy payment terms, and prepare a startup lite[1] friendly version.

The first step may be the hardest, but if it's the **only** step taken (as in no second step), it's rather fruitless. Instead, I urge you to lift your head from the weeds to focus on the bigger picture: the *why* versus the *how*. And once you do, it will guide your entire journey from there on.

Want to know where you're heading? Just follow the money....

HOW AN INFOGRAPHIC CHANGED MY LIFE

Who knew an infographic had the power to change anything?!

A while back, I was perusing an infographic[2] on startup funding.

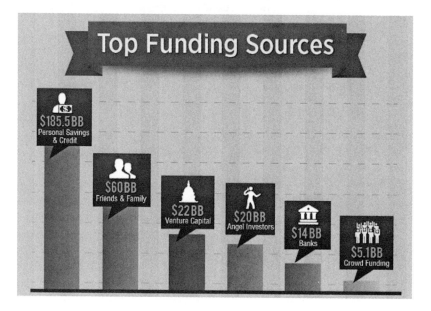

Figure 9.1 - Top Funding Sources

When looking at the funding sources, you might expect the lion's share of investment to be coming from the venture capital (VC) and/or angel investor community. I know I certainly did. Turns out, the VC and angel contributions are only 14 percent of the total funding pie, covering less than 1 percent of total startups. Talk about a lopsided distribution.

The majority of dollars and an average of just under $79,000 comes from "personal savings and credit," combined with "friends and family." Together, they make up a staggering 81 percent of total funding, covering 95 percent of all startups.

THE RUB

The overwhelming majority of startups will never get fully funded...they will fail. They will run out of funding. They will go out of business.

We kind of already knew that 93 percent+ of startups will fail, and yet this astronomical failure rate does not even remotely dampen the dream—not just the American Dream, but a Global Dream—to quit your day job and pursue your mission of changing the world or taking down Goliath.

What hit home for me was a very dark, sobering, ugly truth: **we are selling the next generation of entrepreneurs on an unrealistic ideal, and, in doing so, putting them on the path to bankruptcy.**

The entire startup ecosystem is built around this inconvenient truth: the entrepreneurial revolution is being funded by the life savings of the dreamers—the crazy ones. The *misfits*. The *rebels*. The troublemakers. The round pegs in the square holes. The ones who see things differently....

...And the shared workspaces, incubators, accelerators, conferences, matchmakers, brokered introductions, and pitch events are all getting rich at the expense of startups. Literally.

The vulture capitalists, on the other hand, selectively wait on the sidelines until they can sink their fangs into the next Uber, AirBnB, or Twitter. And even they have an incredibly poor success-to-failure ratio, but trust me...they're not crying poverty.

I'm not saying the system is necessarily broken. I just think it could better, and improved upon. This has become my North Star, my mission: **to reduce the failure rate of startups by even 1 percent**. If I could play a direct role in putting more money back into the pockets of the real heroes (and their friends and family who aren't talking to them anymore), and indirectly influence countless others to do the same, imagine the wealth creation—or redistribution—that could take place, and the positive impact it could have on so many lives!

And the good news is, I know just where to start....

MONEY. MONEY. MONEY.

Money makes the world go round. This is true in the startup world, as well. In the venture world, people talk about smart versus dumb money. According to Venture Hacks, smart money is money plus the promise of help that's worth paying for; dumb money is money plus hidden harm. Both definitions, however, refer to the same pool of funding: angel investor and venture capitalists.

If you ever want to treat yourself to an ethnographical slice of the financial or fundraising side of the startup, just go to breakfast at the famous Rosewood Hotel on Sand Hill Road. There, you'll see carbon copy after carbon copy of startup founders leaning forward to match the profile of a silver haired, jeans-and-open-collared-shirt-wearing V.C. They're all having the exact same conversation about the exact same things: term sheets, cap tables, EBITDA, revenue streams, monetization, and exit strategies.

But what if there were a new source of money, and with it, a new set of benefits?

If it's true that startups have ideas but no money, and brands have money but no ideas, doesn't it make sense that the two sides should be talking to one another? Doesn't it seem logical enough that the two extreme opposites could, in fact, be perfect partners?

It's a mistake to assume every startup founder wants to become the next Zuck. What if money isn't the sole motivator? Or power? Or status—it's complicated! What if it's just about making the world a better place? Or seeing your baby born? Or witnessing a dream become a reality? Or, quite pragmatically, paying down the mortgage on your home?

My advice to the startup community goes along these lines: *you'll never be the next Instagram, but you'd be perfect for Stella Artois!*

At the other end of the spectrum, you have the corporate world. Remember the statement about large companies having more money than brains? Well, this is where all of that money comes into play. Come on, surely you can see how the teensiest tiniest sliver of the $580 billion+ could be put to better use?

To be clear, I'm referring to going big or going home. I'm referring to investing or acquiring startups, though I might as well 鮃等商唄逐權利承認 [3] because it is still so much easier to sell through a $4.5 million Super Bowl spot than it is to spend $45,000 on a well-structured blockchain test. Can you imagine if you were given $4.5 million to spend on blockchain? Would you even know what to do? Could you even spend all that money?

I am reminded of a General Motors executive who, back in 2006, asked me what the company should do with respect to the "blogosphere." I replied, "Well, you could buy it!"

THE BRIEF

When a startup founder gives me their elevator pitch, I love it when there is a personal connection to the product itself. "As a mom, I could never find one central resource to help plan a birthday party—from invitations to booking venues and entertainment, from ordering the cake and goodie bags to taking photos, etc., so I created brthd.ay (beta)."

Startup founders in general have a certain ever-present curiosity, and, more often than not, are connected to a particular pain point.

Hey, did you hear the one about the surfer who wanted to capture his surfing exploits, but didn't have a camera crew on retainer (and besides, he wanted to capture it from his first-person shooting vantage point)? So he started the world's fastest and best-selling camera, GoPro, and fortunately did it before the advent of drones!

And then it hit me: don't companies have these same pain points? The same frustrations? Even the same curiosity? Of course they do. They have so many:

- We suck
- We have a terrible product, and the only way to sell it is through misleading advertising
- Millennials hate us
- We're losing market share
- Our lunch is being stolen by startups

Corporations are full of it. By *it*, I mean challenges. They are actually very, very good at expressing these challenges. They put it in the form of a brief. A creative brief. A neat, standardized, and sanitized précis of their monster problems.

You would think that with this fantastic document in hand, the perfect solution would follow nicely and naturally.

You would be wrong.

For some reason, when entrepreneurs go through this exercise (albeit informally, and without a written brief), they end up using technology to create a kickass, tech-based solution. However, when big brands do it, they end up with advertising! Or a Real-Time Tweet!

WHAT IF?

Collaborating with startups is the essence of digital disruption: creating a new source of funding, and, in doing so, ensuring that great ideas with great potential survive and thrive is a big idea. Here's an even bigger one: *If most startups go out of business, and those that actually make it end up on Madison Avenue's doorstop hawking underwhelming, outdated, and uninspiring sponsorship opportunities, what if the process BEGAN at Madison Avenue's doorstep versus ENDING there?*

By reverse-engineering the startup from the brand backward, technology solutions could be tailor-made to solve real business problems.

There would be no need for inter-media-ries, namely middlemen.

By becoming investors <u>and</u> inventors, brands could reinvent marketing, and in doing so, could be part of the solution of providing utility and service to their customers and community versus adding to the existing problem of clutter, noise, apathy, and irrelevance.

AND SO I ASKED THE QUESTION, "WHAT IF?"

What if Kodak had acquired Instagram? Might they have survived?

What if Blockbuster had invested in Netflix when they had the chance?

What if Marriott had started AirBnB??

The list goes on and on....

In 1998, Kodak had 170,000 employees, and sold 85 percent of all photo paper worldwide. In just three years, taking photos on film completely disappeared, and they went bankrupt.

Kodak was actually a pioneer in digital photography, proving that first isn't always best. Digital cameras were actually invented in 1975!

And to answer the question (which was rhetorical, but whatever...): *if Kodak had acquired Instagram, the reality is that they would have royally fucked it up!* They would have squeezed out every last bit of entrepreneurial juice as they attempted to force-fit Instagram filters into their 400 ISO film. Instagram wouldn't have been their first rodeo. They actually purchased a cool startup called Ofoto in 2001, and in true corporate suckage fashion, renamed it the Kodak EasyShare Gallery in 2005. *Rolls off the tongue, don't it?*

That might be so, but I'd bet if Kodak could do it all over again, they'd do it differently. Hindsight is 20/20, especially against the backdrop of bankruptcy.

Speaking of which, Blockbuster didn't even get to the point where they *could* bastardize Netflix, because they passed on the opportunity to acquire them. They couldn't get out of their own way. Corporate arrogance translated into wagging a fat finger at the young buck, chiding, "You're not big enough! Come back to us when you have reach!" The young startup smiles sheepishly and says, "I'll come back, all right...to kick *you* to the curb faster than you can say *late fee!*"

Want one more "What if?" I'll take your silence as a yes.

What if Gillette had bought Dollar Shave Club? They didn't. Unilever did!

Gillette was pretty much a monopoly. Unchallenged in their market leadership in the men's grooming space. With celebrity endorsers like Tiger Woods, Ryan Lochte, and Ray Rice, what could go wrong?

As political satirist and comedian Bill Maher would say, *"I don't know this for a fact; I just know it's true."* That's how I imagine a boardroom scene in which Dollar Shave Club founder Michael Dubin went in bright-eyed and bushy-tailed, hoping to get some funding or partnership from Gillette and/or parent Procter & Gamble, only to be escorted out by security!

So DSC produced (what is now referred to as an iconic/gold standard example of content marketing) an irreverent video, which duly put them on the map. Before anyone knew it, Schick had been deposed as the #2 razorblade provider in the market.

Part of the Dollar Shave charm was the challenger-brand approach. Everybody loves rooting for David to kick the shins of the slumbering Goliath, taking aim right between the eyes of what once represented a sacrosanct leadership position. *They've been lying to you, bucko! You don't need to change your blades as often as your undies. That's just a marketing ruse!* This wasn't simply style in the form of attitude, tonality, and personality; there was undeniable substance in the form of a **digital**-first, **disruptive** business proposition:

1. a direct-to-consumer subscription model

2. offering a continuous, repeatable revenue stream

3. disintermediation of the established distribution channel

Gillette's response? The ® and ™ -heavy, low-cost Gillette® on Demand.™ Here's some free advice, Gillette: instead of worrying about protecting your fading intellectual property, focus on upgrading your website, because it sucks. It's amazing to see how a once-omnipotent market leader has now become an impotent follower. Double-fault. Game, set, and match to Dubin. Sorry, Mr. Federer.

Or perhaps I got the whole story completely wrong. Let's say it went the other way, with humble Gillette courting arrogant Dollar Shave, begging them to partner, but coming up empty when the greedy startup founder slapped on a few too many zeros on the purchase price—until a sucker eventually came along ready (and desperate enough) to pay the price of a billion dollars.

Even if this *were* true, a billion dollars would have been worth paying (or even overpaying) for the belle of the ball. The opportunity cost of the opportunity lost to a direct competitor, coupled with the time it would take to emulate or find another player (perhaps Harry's?) should be enough to fill in the valuation delta.

In one stroke (using a shaving analogy), or perhaps I should say a billion strokes, Unilever upgraded its position in men's grooming from zero to hero with its purchase of Dollar Shave Club.

Or what if Gillette had started Dollar Shave themselves? Yes, I know hindsight is 20/20, but it *is* possible to teach yourself to "imagine and create the future" and do it like a lean startup (you'll see that later in the Survival Planning chapter.) I've seen it happen. It begins with embracing your heresy, which asks you if you're prepared to put yourself out of business—and it continues with digital disruption that does exactly that!

THE CURIOUS CASE OF RUN PEE

Have you ever been to a movie and desperately needed to go to the bathroom? Of course you have. Everyone has. Think back to the last time it happened, and the dueling feelings of regret (why on Earth did I purchase the monster-sized Coke?), the anxiety (what if I miss the really good parts of the movie?) and the potential humiliation (what if I pee in my pants?)

Introducing Run Pee, a mobile app that will tell you exactly when you can pee during any movie—in other words, the boring part of the movie. Take Marvel's *The Avengers,* for example. The first pee time is at 40 minutes, when Ultron says to Peter, "*You and I can hurt them. But you will tear them apart, from the inside.*"

There's also a detailed synopsis that explains exactly what you missed when you come back to your seat. Moreover, there's a timer that vibrates ahead of each pee time to give you enough notice to plan your pee break accordingly. And if you still needed any more convincing that this app is not directly sent from heaven, you have Apple Watch functionality.

Figure 9.2 - The Run Pee Story

RunPee came from "pain," just like every other great startup ideal. In this case, we're talking about sitting through Peter Jackson's *King Kong*, which was a "bladder-bursting" three hours long.

Who is Run Pee's brand soulmate? Here's a list of suitable suitors:

- Astellas, the parent company of Myrbetriq, a drug that helps with overactive bladder syndrome (OAB)

- AARP. Hey, when you get older, you need to go more frequently.

- Procter & Gamble, which places pretty significant premiums on coveted pregnant moms-to-be and parents of young kids

- Coca-Cola. Yes, you **can** order the Big Gulp!

Now, Astellas did advertise on the app, but why rent when you can own? Furthermore, P&G actually purchased another urinary-themed public restroom finder app called Sit or Squat for its Charmin toilet paper brand, but has done very little with it since (shocking, I know.)

Is it possible the marketing folk over at Myrbetriq (and their myriad agencies) could have conceived this idea themselves? Surely, with the right brief, they could have arrived at the same outcome using a digital disruption lens as their rubric and survival as their North Star? In Chapter 13, I'll show you how this might have been possible.

How is it possible that Run Pee's Chief Peetime Officer, Dan Florio (@polyGeek on Twitter) figured this out, but Myrbetriq and its competitors could not?

Tolterodine is marketed by Pfizer in Canada. Pfizer has approximately 100,000 employees. Just playing the odds would tell you that there has to be at least one employee in that company who suffers from OAB, and/or one entrepreneur that could have thought along these lines. Maybe they are one and the same!

Every single company and every single brand can follow a similar process, and arrive at their own unique and disruptive digital solution. In fact, I guarantee it!

So if this is true, why have so few have succeeded? The answer: Premature evacuation.

No endurance. No patience. No cojones.

CORPORATE TONGUE-TWISTERS: INSTITUTIONALIZING INNOVATION AT AN ENTERPRISE LEVEL

At dinner with a chief marketing officer of a large company, we were discussing pain points and a commensurate digital disruption wish list. *"We need to institutionalize innovation at an enterprise level,"* she directed. I heard her loud and clear. I was all over it. Her brief was sound. She needed a process in place to be able to implement, optimize, scale, and evolve innovation beyond the one-off. She needed a playbook.

A few weeks later, she lost her head of innovation to Starbucks. Shortly after that, she was rotated to run another division within the company. A year or so later, she was rotated <u>back</u> to the same chief marketing officer role. I'm still waiting for "the dust to settle," as per her e-mail response to me so we can catch up and share the recommendations I put together for her. I will not name names, but I will send a signed copy of my book to her with a nice Post-it note on this exact page!

For what it's worth, I suspect that by the time this book comes out, she will have been rotated once again...perhaps even out of the organization entirely!

M.E.T.H.O.D.O.F.L.O.V.E

Our chief marketing officer may have been institutionalized, but that doesn't mean her sacrifice has to have been in vain. Her missing playbook isn't as elusive as you might think. The key is decoding the rules of engagement: translating corporate speak (corporatese) into startup language (English). Fortunately, there is a cipher, and it is all about one word: failure.

I come with a very simple 2x2 matrix to evaluate your adventures in digital disruption in every pilot, partnership, or even purchase.

	Loss	Win
Big	1. *Discountinue*	4. Scale with Success
Small	2. Pivot	3. Rinse 'n' Repeat

Discountinue (the big L as in "Loss")

Recognizing how the word *failure* immediately makes you break out in hives, it's quite apparent we need to figure out one of two paths:

1.   Figure out how to deal with failure (I'll tackle this in the next pillar.)

2.   Reframe the entire notion of failure (read on.)

Nobody likes a loser, but I would argue that the only loser at innovation is the hamstrung person too afraid to fail. In this category or quadrant, you tried something new, and it flatlined.

Give yourself a free pass. You're going to be fine, especially if the stakes were low. How do you know when the stakes were low? Simple. The cost was low, or you were early enough in the game. Doing things ahead of your competition is a real and valuable form of first-mover advantage, EVEN with a negative or underwhelming outcome. Doing things when you *can* versus when you *have to* is getting a discount on the future as opposed to a premium or a tax. Seth Godin said *advertising is the tax we pay for being unremarkable.* Well, experimentation is the **discount** we receive for being innovative. This is why the typo in the word *discountinue*, is, in fact, intentional.

> "Experimentation is the discount we receive for being innovative. "

As far as the meaning goes, "discountinue" speaks to a recommended course of action. If it doesn't work out, don't do it again. Move on, and live to fight another day.

PIVOT (THE SMALL "L")

When I'm mentoring startup founders, I run them through a fun series of really famous pivots:

- Dodgeball, a location-based social networking mobile app, became known as FourSquare

- Odeo began as a podcast directory and pivoted to become Twitter

- The Point, which lived in the intersection of social activism meets crowd wisdom, became Groupon

- Fabulis, a social networking site for gay men, became a curated selection of unexpected men's, women's, home, art, and tech accessories from the world's most exciting designers...known today as Fab

- YouTube began as a dating site where single guys could upload video "pitches" of themselves! "We thought dating would be the obvious choice," said co-founder Steve Chen. After five days, no one had uploaded a single video, so they changed course.

- And then there's Burbn, which was essentially Yelp for restaurants. People would recommend and review their most and least favorite restaurants and meals. The business was chugging along satisfactorily until one day (founder Kevin Systrom actually calls this day "pivot day"), the company came together to talk about what really rocked and what really sucked about the service. The data did not lie. Really, nothing about the site was producing any significant uptick or growth, except for one specific functionality: people were uploading photos of their food at alarming rates and commenting on it with hashtags like #foodporn. There and then, the company discarded its entire business model in order to focus exclusively on photos...of food...clouds.....sex (all porn) and in fact anything else you can imagine. Instagram was born!

In the digital disruption world, pivoting is the equivalent of the small "l" for loss. Things didn't work out as you planned, but that's totally fine. If at first you don't succeed, try, try again.

Failure is the cost of doing business in the world of digital disruption, and the absence of it is pretty much a guarantee of...failure.

Sometimes, pivoting is easy. For example, if you have a choice of three different approaches and one doesn't work, just move on to number two—and, if necessary, number three. That's the common-sense approach. For some reason, in the corporate world, this approach does not compute. Everyone bolts faster than Usain. It's quite remarkable how a small, self-contained experiment could be looked at as failure when all around, the company is imploding on itself. With a pivot or two, it could quite possibly be the cure!

Here's a twist on the optimist-pessimist, glass-half-full/empty adage. An entrepreneur sees a partially shattered empty glass, and thanks to his or her reality distortion field, passion, vision, masochism, and stubbornness, has the belief and faith that not only will it once again be full, but that it will, in fact, overflow.

Go back to the well. Move a couple of things around. Even change your partner if you have to, but whatever you do...don't give up. If you do nothing, you are only moving backward.

RINSE 'N' REPEAT (THE SMALL "w")

Play it again, Sam. If you see what I call *proof of life*—in other words, a key indicator being roused from its chronic slumber and bursting into giddy life as it dances up the charts—why walk away from what could be a big bet?

"One and done" is nothing more than a P.R. stunt, and unless you're doing something substantial, like sending a Tesla into space courtesy of my countryman, Elon Musk, I would caution you against looking at digital disruption as an isolated tactic to cross off your never-ending checklist.

There are several ways to rinse and repeat: from literally repeating it again without changing a thing (your sample size has increased from n=1 to n=2), to changing a single variable (like bringing in another business unit, brand, or geographic market) to adding a bit more spike to the punch in the form of incremental increases in budget, scope, complexity, or functionality.

Establishing momentum is key. Everyone wants hockey-stick growth, but no one wants to *stick* around to wait for the afterburners to kick in. Like the days of "viral marketing" mania and the desperation of companies to crack the secret formula of viral success: instant hits, just add memes.

SCALE WITH SUCCESS (THE BIG "W")

From *discountinue* to *pivot* to *rinse and repeat*, it's all been leading up to this: the big one. The big fish. The diamond in the rough. The baby unicorn. In other words, when something works really, really well, it's finally time to bet the farm, or at least the farmhouse. I've come up with an ever-expanding list that has 15 different scenarios in it. The general idea is simple: if you're in a legacy, sputtering, backfiring, or retarding business (in other words, all businesses), this is your cue to double or triple down on transferring knowledge, talent, time, networks, partners, and, most importantly, money to any project that has the potential for transformation.

Investment and even **acquisition** are at the top of this list.

Just as timing is an art form, so, too, is investing. Knowing when to ante up, pull back, or double down is key. Here's a litmus test for you to follow: imagine you open up the newspaper in the morning and find out your direct competitor purchased the same company before you. How do you feel? Did you miss out on the opportunity of a lifetime because you dragged your feet, or did you dodge a bullet?

In pressing times of constant budget cuts, my advice is simple: get the money any legal way you can! Find another budget in your organization by opening up your *precious* idea to another executive sponsor. It might mean letting go of control somewhat, but it will be worth it. In the investment world, I guess they would call that dilution.

And if all else fails, I say this: go outside. If you truly care about your company, you'll approach friends and family, angels, and VCs, or commit an act of true heresy and partner up with *other* brand organizations—even competitors of yours.

THE SECRET OF SUCCESS

You're in luck. There actually **is** a formula for success, and I'll share it with you, but I'm not sure you're going to love it entirely.

As I tell entrepreneurs, "Your success depends on four factors: two you can control, and two you cannot."

The controllables are the *idea* and the *execution* of that idea; the uncontrollables are *timing* and *luck*. I think you get the former two, so I'll just focus on the latter two components.

Just because things work today, doesn't mean they will work tomorrow. Conversely, just because things don't work today, doesn't mean they won't work tomorrow.

Cases in point: MySpace, Google Glass, and QR Codes. Poor idea? Poor execution? Or just poor timing?

Oftentimes, people, ideas, companies, and technology are ahead of their time, and unless they have enough runway to tread water and bide their time, they'll probably be *out of time*.

Timing is an art form, and often as much a function of luck (dumb, beginner's, calculated) as a learned skill. I heard the co-founder of Netscape and VC Firm Andreessen-Horowitz, Marc Andreessen once say that if every single failed dot com from the infamous bubble of 2000/2001 were to have started up in recent times, every single one of them would have succeeded!

What about luck? I use two quotes to illustrate this:

1. Luck is what happens when preparation meets opportunity. In an interview with the king of all media, Howard Stern, CBS *The Late Show*'s Stephen Colbert was talking about his success as the newly crowned number #1 in late-night, doing something that his predecessor, the great David Letterman, could never achieve against his nemesis Jay Leno. In this interview, he rejected the notion that Donald Trump was the reason for his success, referencing his nightly barrage of scathing indictments against the President. Instead, he spoke about how he and his team had been preparing for this moment, and regardless of the outcome of the election, they were prepared to take advantage of their hard work and preparation.

2. As my other countryman, Gary Player, likes to say, "The more I practice, the luckier I get." This statement could have been used to explain the "viral video" craze. While it was nearly impossible to predict or produce viral success on a consistent basis, certain production companies seemed to get it right more often than not. In a funny way, this really is no different from being an entrepreneur today: *if at first you don't succeed, try...try...try again.* What a great way to describe the art of failure!

My son's football or soccer (depending on which side of the pond you sit) club has a motto: control the controllables. Max out on the things you can control versus stressing about the things you can't. That's why rinsing and repeating is so important. You'll never get comfortable with the fluidity and unpredictability of innovation if you don't look at it as a continuous process.

If sucking less is to become a reality, digital disruption needs to be an ongoing way of life and corporate culture.

MARKETING AS A REVENUE GENERATOR

One of the obvious ways of making the shift from marketing as a cost center or expense to that of a revenue generator is to rethink its very role. Marketing has (or should have) a complete monopoly on the consumer in terms of understanding how he thinks; how she acts; what makes them tick; what makes them buy. Consumer insights, research, the voice of the customer, focus groups, and social media listening provide a powerful combination of insights into motivation, behavior change, perception, attitudes, and preference. So why not monetize that?

Ritz Carlton did this when they began to charge other companies for their secret sauce of customer experience leadership.

Dell did it when they productized their social media command centers and helped other companies learn firsthand how much they really sucked.

Think bigger!

Why wouldn't corporations mind-meld with the investment community to produce real multiples of revenue in return? The world of venture capital should not be the only sector capable of producing big-time exits. If a company buys into a startup, and helps it get to the next level and scale by integrating it into the brand's overall go-to market proposition and customer base, why shouldn't it consider an early-stage exit or "flip?" With the backing of the corporation, the startup is now even more attractive to subsequent investors, and it certainly bodes well for its independence by successfully detaching from the mothership.

To me, this is so obvious. I hope it is to you, as well.

A FINAL WORD

A gaggle of geese. A swarm of bees. A parliament of owls. What about lemmings? Popular belief is the collective noun is *slice*, but some refer to a *suicide* of lemmings. This is also an *apropos* way to describe corporate executives when it comes to the way they blindly follow, follow, follow one another over the (bleeding) edge of the cliff.

So, before you get too gung-ho about leaping from one extreme to the other, a word of caution to make sure you don't leave your common sense at the door.

CASE IN POINT: THE RUSH TO OPEN INNOVATION.

On the surface, open innovation is the perfect example of building external partnerships with tech-enabled businesses: the very definition of digital disruption.

It would appear that nowadays, the concept of open innovation is all the rage, and therein lies the problem. There's too much superficiality, and too many unrealistic and lopsided partnership beliefs—from onerous legal terms and conditions to unfair ownership of IP to ridiculous expectations of solving multi-billion-dollar industry challenges and corporate woes with shoestring budgets.

How would you counter the public perception that we utilize death squads to take care of opposition to our ongoing water-pillaging efforts?

There's also the strategic disconnect of the open approach. In a hyper-competitive world, why on earth would you telegraph your biggest challenges and pain points to the entire world and your nearest and dearest competitors?

Whether we're talking about open innovation or *any kind* of digital disruption collaboration or partnership, build these bonds and foster the kind of relationships that will endure. If earned media impressions, awards, or press interviews are your barometers of success, you are probably compensating for something.

CHAPTER 10

TALENT RESURRECTION

I N THE PREVIOUS CHAPTER, I INTRODUCED THE CONCEPT OF DIGItal disruption as a means of finally utilizing digital in the way it was always meant to be used—namely, as a transformative, disruptive force. The path to this process involves forging immutable bonds and connections with entrepreneurs outside of the company.

Looking outside the company, however, is only one part of the solution. After all, there's no point of doing business if you have no employees left to help you.

It's time to look inward and harness the untapped power within your failing organization. Yes, power. More than you could imagine. I'm referring to the second pillar: your ultimate internal capability—your talent—and the ability to resurrect it from the mortuary slab.

Sadly, necromancy is not one of the skills endorsed on your LinkedIn profile, especially when you're dealing with a broken, flawed, and inefficient culture, system, process, and morale.

CHARITY BEGINS AT HOME

As in the previous chapter, the goal here is not to scrape by, doing the bare minimum to stay afloat for as long as possible. This is about winning the talent war, which is unfortunate, as you're most likely losing it...if you haven't lost it already.

For those of you who haven't given up, think about talent resurrection through this simple lens:

1. INPUT: attracting and retaining talent

2. OUTPUT: harnessing the power of that talent

3. OUTCOME: cultural change that begins from within

Young talent is in short supply nowadays. Millennials and their Z counterparts just don't want to be working at behemoths. They don't need Gold Rolexes upon retirement, though they might settle for a diamond-studded Apple Watch! If you happen to have one of them working at your company today, I would recommend shackling them to their cube ASAP, because it's probably a *fait accompli* they won't be there tomorrow. Most likely, they'll be headhunted by a tech company or quit to start their own startup...maybe even a startup capable of taking down the very company that initially buttered their bread. How's that for *chutzpah*?

By 2020, the first millennials will turn 40. They will also make up 40 percent of the population by 2020, which will make them the largest segment.

80 percent of them will be married. For starters, it's time to stop thinking of millennials as pimply-faced, self-entitled brats still living with their folks!

They will make up 35 percent[1] of the global workforce, with Gen Z making up another 24 percent. That's a combined 59 percent of the workforce aged 40 or younger, and 100 percent of them won't be working for you!

To be clear, this talent attrition epidemic is not limited to the youngsters. Over the course of my consulting career, almost every senior marketer (client or otherwise) I've come into contact with cries me a river about their job dissatisfaction, job search, and job opportunities outside of their current one.

Let me repeat that in a different way: just about every executive <u>and</u> the direct reports in your organization are looking for another job right now!

And if you deny the fact that **you're** looking, as well, you are only lying to yourself.

THE ROOT CAUSE: LACK OF ENTREPRENEURIAL ETHOS

Your institution does not foster creative or entrepreneurial thinking because you are in the risk mitigation versus risk management business.

You discourage and punish failure, while rewarding mediocrity and monotony.

You are in the business of standard operating best practices: following an anal playbook to the letter versus encouraging free, radical thinking. This flies in the face of the entrepreneur and how they problem-solve.

And until you solve this, your company will continue to hemorrhage talent.

THE DEATH OF CORPORATE MONOGAMY

To have any chance of making it, companies need to embrace—even encourage—corporate polygamy. Moonlighting, freelancing, or, as Uber calls it, "side hustle," is integral to keeping employees engaged and motivated.

Think about it for a moment. Do you really think your W2 salaried work-force loves you so much they would tattoo your logo on their bodies? Why is it that a customer of yours might deface their bodies with your logo and yet your employees, who sacrifice their blood, sweat, and tears to help pay off your chairman's third private jet, don't go there? How do you expect them to be *lifers* when you are an "at-will" employer? When you are not ready to reciprocate the loyalty and give them tenure? When you don't incentivize them for ideas and compensate them accordingly? When your culture punishes employees for sticking out their necks and thinking entrepreneur-ially on behalf of your business?

The single biggest contributor to corporate decay is a talent-centric one. It's actually quite obvious. People run companies (at least until the machines take over). Human resource departments right now are the only ones standing between the chasm of nirvana and purgatory. Sadly, they have become part of the problem; once a friend and confidant of the employee, they have now become financial and legal-affairs lackeys and henchmen.

Not surprisingly, the only innovation within talent design has come from the startup community. I've done a fair amount of work in this category, and uncovered enough startup accelerants and catalysts of change to convince me that all is not lost. All it takes now is for corporations to give them a chance! There is an incredibly fertile proving ground out there, but are you prepared to venture out of your comfort zones to rewrite the corporate HR playbook? The stakes are too high not to....

TIME TO RETURN THOSE HERMAN MILLER CHAIRS

I'm actually sitting on one right now. I bought it on eBay from a failed dot com circa 2002/2003. Looks like there'll be a glut of supply in the months and years to come, including—but not limited to—standing desks, treadmill desks, beanbags, or whatever corporations thought would entice those young'uns to work for them in the future.

If the central premise of this book is that corporations have lost their competitive edge, then it stands to reason that the most important thing for these corporations to do is figure out how to get their groove back.

Luring talent by overpaying and underworking them (because didn't you hear, millennials are lazy, demanding, and self-entitled?) may still not be enough to prevent losing them to the Googles, Facebooks, and newly rising startups out there.

YOU CAN'T AUTOMATE STUPID

If you think the answer lies in replacing them with machines, that's not exactly a winning strategy, either. Fewer people is not the solution. Just look at Apple's Genius Bars as a reminder of the power of humanity. Rather, focus on fixing the revolving door and culture of continuous talent attrition.

Enough Bashing. Time for a Solution!

Step one on the road to recovery is to create a climate and culture of what I call *stable volatility* or even *volatile stability*. Volatile stability is essentially creating a safe and secure place to fuck up constantly. Where the only constant is change. Where failure is baked into the DNA of the company.

Figure 10.1 - Decline into Obsolescence Courtesy of Marketoonist

Business as usual today is anything but. The instability of the world *outside* the corporation needs to be carefully balanced *inside*, with an environment that does not have to be safe or play it safe. It does, however, need to be consistent and manage expectations accordingly. Your people don't need more crap in their lives. They get it from their families. They get it from their in-laws. They get it from the government. They get it from the Russians posing as Americans on Facebook. They get it from life. Period. Do they really need more angst and *agita* from the company that keeps them?

Competition is healthy, but it really isn't (or shouldn't be) welcome within a company. Collaboration needs to prevail and replace backstabbing, in-fighting, butt-kissing, and spoon-feeding. If you want to survive, you'll need to all band together and be near perfect in your performance.

One of the best ways not to make a mistake is *not to make a mistake*—and by mistake, I refer to the concept of failure, or dealing with failure. Legendary American football coach Vince Lombardi said, "*We didn't lose the game; we just ran out of time.*" Now, I'm sure you know that famous quote, but did you know Lombardi was an entrepreneur? Failure is inextricably linked to entrepreneurship, and entrepreneurship is inextricably linked to survival. When every entrepreneur goes to work knowing this day could be his or her last, it creates a determination and will to succeed like no other. It also creates a pragmatic acceptance of the inevitability of death, and in a weird sort of way, that's kind of comforting. Especially when there is "life after death" in the form of a pivot or even more radical business shift.

ENTREPRENEURIAL REINCARNATION

The inevitability of death is pretty grim. But what if you knew beyond a shadow of a doubt that there *was* life after death; that there is a better place after you die (unless we're talking about politicians, in which case, you're *definitely* going to hell.) What if you knew you would come back and get another shot at redemption? Another crack at "the game of life?" Would that change your outlook and approach? I'd bet it would.

Sadly, I can't divulge what I really know about life after death due to an NDA I previously signed with the big man upstairs. What I *can* tell you is that entrepreneurs think of failure like you would think of oxygen. It's all around us. It's part of life. It's essential for life. You might take it for granted, but whatever you do, if you starve yourself of it, you will be done.

I recall listening to a VC talk about his acid test for a founder, hoping to get some of his money.

"How many times have you failed?"

"In my life?"

"No, TODAY!"

Alberto Savoia describes himself as an apex innovator at large. Before that, he worked at a startup called Google, where he was an innovation agitator. While there, he developed a practice called *pretotyping* (like prototyping, only much earlier, cheaper, and scrappier in process), and helped executives understand how easy it was to put some form or flesh into an otherwise ephemeral idea to get instant validation and invaluable feedback from key constituents and the desired market. Alberto's words about failure stuck with me: *"I'm not saying you should reward failure, but you certainly should not punish it."* They made me realize that our inability to deal with imperfection will ultimately be our Achilles heel.

"The inability for us to deal with imperfection will ultimately be our Achilles heel."

Done is better than perfect is the rallying cry of the entrepreneur. The corporate executive responds with a pithy, but ultimately pathetic, *nail before we scale*.

Corporations today are too afraid to fail, and thus, they are too afraid to try. The product of this is a form of corporate paralysis that leaves companies hamstrung, handicapped, and held back from moving forward. It also creates a perfect opening for upstarts, challengers, and dreamers to ride this slipstream of corporate inaction to competitive nirvana.

I have quoted Alberto's line so many times, but it strikes me: I'm not sure I agree with the second part of his statement. I believe we *should* reward failure. We should encourage it and embrace it. Literally. Put an awards show together.

Create the *Riskies* or some epigrammatic brand to acknowledge awards like biggest risk taken, biggest lesson learned, most audacious attempt, and biggest advantage gained. The awards could be giant copper or lead Ls (as in L for Loser). Make it as big and bold as you like with various categories, voting, celebrity judges, and, of course, a master of ceremonies.

THANKS. I'D BE DELIGHTED TO HOST.

Remember this: in baseball, if you bat lifetime .333, you're a shoe-in for the Hall of Fame. For all you non-baseballers, .333 or 33% implies they were successful (got to base) 1 out of every 3 attempts. Can you imagine if your corporate culture embraced striking out 2 out of every 3 attempts?

This is all part of the journey to cultural change.

> "The journey to success begins with failure."

BUILT TO FAIL

To be clear, failing for the sake of failing is dumb. No one sets out to fail on purpose. Sure, there are lessons learned, but as former President George W. Bush once said, "You see...a fooled man ain't gonna be fooled again. He he he." That might have been a Will Ferrell impersonation of him, but still....

It's also important to distinguish between types of failure. There are many kinds of failure. You're looking for the *good* kind of failure. The kind that incorporates one or more of the following attributes:

- **Quick.** Get out quick, get back in quicker.

- **Cheap.** When stakes are low, and cost is even lower.

- **Early.** "When you can" as opposed to "when you have to."

- **Conduit.** A means to an end.

- **Catalyst.** Spurring bigger thinking and better results.
- **Competitive**. Before the rest of the lemmings pile on.

I believe we need to rethink (and ultimately rebrand) the word "fail" and its very meaning. If to a hammer, everything is a nail, then to a consultant, everything is an acronym. So here's mine: **Finally Acknowledge Insights & Learnings (F.A.I.L.)**

For good measure, here are some other popular ones:

- First Attempt in Learning
- Flawlessly Ascending in Life
- Found Another Interesting Lesson
- Future Always Involves Learning

VOLATILE STABILITY IS NOT FOR EVERYONE

Actually, it's probably not for anyone. As humanoids, our brains are programmed to find order from chaos; to envelop ourselves with the comfort foods of normalcy, predictability, and routine. We follow the same morning routines, drive the same way to work, order the same triple decaf/no-foam, no-soy, no-taste lattes from Starbucks. We actually thrive on routine—and even monotony.

That might cut it into our personal lives, but it simply won't do in a business environment. Sure, consistency is the hallmark of building an enduring global brand—which is a contradiction—but not if you're consistently bad or consistently worse than your competitors, or consistently under-delivering against your customers' expectations.

As a rule of thumb, anytime you get a little too comfortable at work, it's time to change things up, but when every single employee is in the same corporate coma, you're going to be in a world of hurt down the line.

Your employees are not going to be inclined to take risks, especially if their company isn't. They aren't queuing up to disrupt the status quo, embrace their heresy, or cannibalize their cash cow. That's just crazy talk. They are more than happy to come in late (or at least 10 seconds before their boss) and leave early, especially when they're not on the clock.

Which is why it's time to ban the employee.

Ban the Employee

Employee.

Noun 1. a person working for another person or a business firm for pay.

Inspirational, huh?

If you're an employee who clocks in daily, you've most likely already checked out, and your days are probably numbered anyway. If dysfunction and political shenanigans aren't going to get you, then automation and artificial intelligence will. Either way, you lose.

Most likely, you're counting down the days until a headhunter or some other company rescues you, only to find S.S.D.D.: Same Shit, Different Day.

Perhaps you'll cut the corporate cord and try your hand at the startup life. After all, you have Kickstarter, Indigogo, *Shark Tank*, and Dragon's Den to help fast-track your rise to the top.

...But what if you could achieve that inside your own company?

If you are a corporation, or even worse, someone who works in human resources (your job will be one of the first the machines come for, thanks to a sundae of artificial intelligence, predictive analytics, virtual reality, and big data that will *automagically* recruit, interview, hire, promote, and even fire #youtoo), it's time to wake up and take stock of two simple truths:

1. Companies will live and die based upon how they attract and retain talent.

2. When it comes to attracting, retaining, engaging, and activating talent, you're 0-4.

It doesn't have to be that way.

If it's true that all the great talent is going to startups, why not at least act like one? Adopt the same cultural principles and practices, especially as they relate to talent. Yes, this involves a radical and arguably impossible cultural transformation, but there has to be a place to start. The first step is often the hardest, but it's also the most empowering.

Fortunately, I can tell you where to start, and put you on the right path. The odds are hugely stacked against you, but miracles do happen, especially with perseverance, hard work, and stubborn resolve. Slowly but surely, you may begin to shed that crusty exterior of your corporate cocoon to reveal the magnificent form of your former self: an entrepreneurial butterfly!

Essentially, *become more entrepreneurial, like you once were.* And a big part of this journey involves your "employees" becoming more entrepreneurial. Or *intrapreneurial.*

Intrapreneur. noun

1. *an employee of a large corporation who is given freedom and financial support to create new products, services, systems, etc., and does not have to follow the corporation's usual routines or protocols.*

Your company's survival depends on your ability to transform your workforce into an entrepreneurial melting pot: a panacea of disruptive ideas capable of cannibalizing your business and discovering new and exciting business models and revenue streams.

TO UNDERSTAND THE ENEMY, BECOME THE ENEMY

In this case, you are already your own worst enemy, and it's not even your fault. In an organization built to suck, the odds were always stacked against you. From the get-go, you were on a crash course to fail. It wasn't always this way; your company was once agile, nimble, lean, and mean. Then it got too big, and collapsed under its own weight.

The company might be chronically or even terminally ill, but that doesn't mean its people have to be. From 30,000 feet, the prognosis doesn't look good at all, but when you look a little deeper, there are a few mavericks, shit-stirrers, and even visionaries waiting for their chance to lead and make a difference. They are typically younger and less experienced, which is not ageist at all. It's just a fact. The reason is simple: they have had less time to be beaten down, beaten up, and beaten into submission.

SIR KEN ROBINSON WILL EXPLAIN

Well over 10 years ago, I had the extreme pleasure of attending a keynote given by Sir Ken Robinson at a Microsoft Strategic Summit in Redmond. This was back in the day when MSN sold online advertising for a living.

> Sir Kenneth Robinson (born March 4, 1950) is a British author, speaker, and international advisor on education in the arts to government, non-profits, and education and arts bodies. Robinson has suggested that to engage and succeed, education must develop on three fronts. First, it should foster diversity by offering a broad curriculum and encourage individualization of the learning process. Second, it should foster curiosity through creative teaching, which depends on high-quality teacher training and development. Finally, it should focus on awakening creativity through alternative didactic processes that put less emphasis on standardized testing, thereby giving the responsibility for defining the course of education to individual schools and teachers.

He believes that much of the current education system in the
United States fosters conformity, compliance, and standardization
rather than creative approaches to learning. Robinson emphasizes that we can only succeed if we recognize that education is an
organic system, not a mechanical one. Successful school administration is a matter of fostering a helpful climate rather than
"command and control."

The WHAT and HOW focus on education (with the corporate parallel being
training), but it's important to touch on the WHO and WHY. Children.
I believe that children are the future. Teach them well, and let them lead the way.[2]
Children are born with unbridled enthusiasm. They know no boundaries or
restrictions. The word *no* does not exist in their dictionaries. Just ask my kids!
They believe they can do anything; accomplish everything; be anyone. When
you ask a kid what they want to be when they grow up, they don't say accoun-
tant, inside sales rep, or warehouse manager; they say astronaut, fireman, fighter
pilot, doctor, scientist, or Elon Musk.

Your "employees" are like children. They have the capacity to do incredible
things in their professional lifetimes. They are smart, qualified, talented, and
beyond capable. After all, you hired them on the basis and strength of these
credentials, right? And of course, their glowing references, which naturally
were all 100 percent positive (because who puts down a reference that is going
to badmouth you out of a job?).

Your employees understand your business as well as you do. Possibly even better
than you do. They live at the rock face. They represent the grassroots. They
operate on the frontlines. They are embodiments of the real business, warts
and all. There is no sanitized, retouched, airbrushed, legal, or corporate-com-
munications-approved version of the truth. They only have their truth. Which
is THE truth.

Which means they hold the key to your future, your survival, and your evolution. They understand exactly how to fix what is broken, how to turn the good into great, or how to just have fucking cool ideas.

And yet you've beaten the crap out of them. Instilled a culture of *incrementalism*, risk aversion, risk mitigation, repression, and even spite.

Which is why they've become the waiters who spit into your soup right before they leave the kitchen for your table. And you deserve it!

Imagine the possibilities if you were able to harness the collective wisdom of your internal crowd. Imagine what kinds of ideas are percolating right this very second, buried and seemingly dormant under the surface of their exterior cubicles. How many of these ideas will see the light of day? Or perhaps I should ask, how many of them will leave the company with these ideas, and end up doing them independently? Perhaps even with your competition? How many of your ex-employees will end up putting *you* out of business?

A study from Freshbooks, a cloud-based accounting company, revealed that the number of self-employed workers could triple by 2020. That translates into 42 million, with millennials leading the way. Freshbooks found that 97% of self-employed workers had no desire to return to traditional work.

The very priorities associated with work are changing. Authority and remuneration are in decline, whereas autonomy and creativity are on the rise.

DON'T GET MAD. AND DON'T GET EVEN.

Instead of embracing this behavioral and cultural sea change, most companies fight it. They get mad...and *then* they try to get even. They look to sue the employee and accuse them of creating their own ideas "on company time." Now, "on company time" embodies everything that's wrong with the corporation. We're talking antiquated and out-of-touch practices that are really just designed to make the lawyers on retainer feel like they're barely doing their jobs.

We expect our talent to be on high alert and answer e-mails on nights and weekends, but they can't pursue their own passions as part of the gig economy? It makes no sense. What sheer hypocrisy, and what a double standard: you don't allow employees to have personal time at work, but you make them work when they're out of the office.

SHIFT HAPPENS

There will always be those who are content to punch in and out on schedule, and you'll always need your fair share of warm bodies around. Unfortunately for you, none of this crop is going to make any significant inroads into the erosion of your chances of survival. I once heard a dumb person being referred to by the snarky name "oxygen invader." So perhaps we should call your model employees "cubicle invaders."

At the other end of the continuum, you have the real difference-makers. The ones that this very second are working on their exit strategy from your company to start their own journey toward a very different kind of exit strategy. At the end of the chapter, I'll tell you how I think you can embrace the heresy of encouraging your employees to pursue their entrepreneurial passions and not lose them in the process.

In the middle, you have a pretty substantial group who are waiting to find purpose, meaning, and the opportunity to truly actualize themselves, because deep down, we're all closeted entrepreneurs (just ask Sir Ken.)

The idea of transforming your workforce from employees to intrapreneurs is a pretty big idea. There is no doubt that this is the way to go.

NATURE VS. NURTURE

I don't believe for a second that people can't be trained to be(come) entrepreneurs. I think it's a colossal failing of the corporation: its principles, practices, worst practices, training, and development (or the lack thereof), and, most importantly, the reward-and-compensation structure that has obviated the realization of a dynamic, evolving, and adaptive corporate organism.

I met Armin Eichhorn at Mondelēz International in Bremen. He was a consultant who had previously worked at Lego. He is no longer there, which is not surprising, and not necessarily a criticism, either. During the time we worked together, he shared a fantastic paper from Saras D. Sarasvathy, Associate Professor at the Darden Graduate School of Business Administration at the University of Virginia, entitled "What Makes Entrepreneurs Entrepreneurial?"

Sarasvathy introduces three types of reasoning: causal, creative causal, and effectual, corresponding to managerial, strategic, and entrepreneurial thinking, respectively.

For purposes of this discussion, the focus will be on causal (what we are taught in business school, a.k.a. book smarts) versus effectual (what we learn by doing, a.k.a. street smarts). Whereas casual reasoning begins with a predetermined goal and a given set of means, and seeks to identify the optimal (fastest, cheapest, most efficient) alternative to achieve a given goal, effectual reasoning does not begin with a specific goal. Instead, it begins with a given set of means, and allows goals to emerge contingently over time.

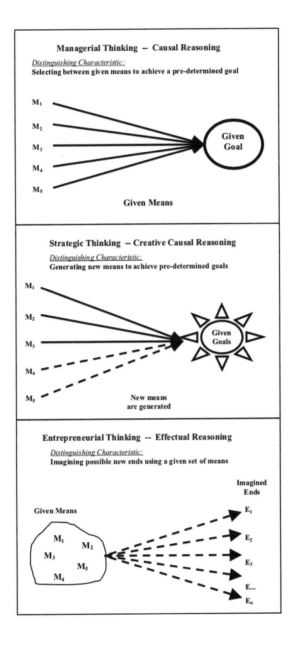

Figure 10.2 - Causal v Effectual Reasoning

Some primary differences between the two are laid out very clearly by Saras-vathy:

1. While causal reasoning focuses on expected return, effectual reasoning emphasizes affordable loss. <u>Affordable loss</u> can be loosely translated into "done is better than perfect."

2. While causal reasoning urges the exploitation of preexisting knowledge and prediction, effectual reasoning stresses the leveraging of contingencies (how you react to them).

3. Unlike causal reasoning, which comes to life through careful planning and subsequent execution, effectual reasoning lives and breathes execution. There is no place for procrastination or *"nail before we scale"* in this world!

4. Causal reasoning is based on the logic: to the extent that we can *predict the future, we can control it.* Effectual reasoning, however, is based on the logic: to the extent that we can control the future, we do not need to predict it. This reminds me of Peter Drucker's saying: *"Defending the past is far riskier than creating the future."*

5. Effectual reasoning may not necessarily increase the probability of success of new enterprises, but it reduces the costs of failure *(discountinue!)* by enabling the failure to occur earlier and at lower levels of investment.

6. *Entrepreneurs are entrepreneurial because they believe in a yet-to-be-made future that can be substantially shaped by human action.* If you ever needed an endorsement for the importance of talent, let this be your guide.

Transforming your employees into entrepreneurs inside isn't just a cultural imperative, it's a business imperative. When your talent becomes a feedback and innovation loop that plugs directly into your growth, customer intimacy, and competitive-advantage workstreams, how can you lose?

That last question was rhetorical, but I'll answer it anyway. You lose by not taking decisive action fast enough around talent/design elements, including—but not limited to—liberal or flexible hiring practices, public recognition, contests and rewards, education, training, and development.

To get you started, here are six approaches that will help you kickstart your efforts to create a culture of entrepreneurship or intrapreneurship inside your company.

1. IMITATION IS THE SINCEREST FORM OF KICKSTARTERY

Investment acceleration engines like Kickstarter and Indigogo have put crowd-funding on the map. Products like the Pebble Watch, Oculus, and the Fidget Cube were all launched using a grassroots micro-funding methodology that utilized rewards and experiential tiers to get to market. The results have been staggering. One of my pipe dreams is to formalize the digital disruption invest-ment pipeline by creating a company that helps corporates invest in startups. Any takers? Contact me.

In this case, however, I'm talking about building the same engine inside the firewalls of the company that give employees—or, should I say aspiring entre-preneurs—the visibility (and, more importantly, the means) to get noticed, voted up, validated, and ultimately funded.

Many companies do elements or aspects of this big vision, but I don't believe they are doing so at the scope, scale, and extent to which I am referring. What I'd like to see is EVERY company doing this in a highly publicized manner, AND doing it right. Employee-centric innovation engines are, at a minimum, growth engines—but really and truly, they are survival engines. They can't be done anemically, sporadically, or half-assed.

Employee-centric innovation engines are, at a minimum, growth engines—but really and truly, they are survival engines.

The visibility angle is important. Naturally, it should be promoted heavily and aggressively inside the company. No point in having yet another white elephant roaming the empty corridors and taking a dump somewhere in the maze of cubicles. The external component is important, as well, as it will have a dual impact of both attracting future employees talent and also pleasing (or temporarily appeasing) shareholders.

Doing it right is all about an unwavering combination of strength, speed, and endurance. Great ideas need to sprint to the finish line. Good ideas can become great over time, and with the right feedback, mentoring, and counseling. Even crap ideas can pivot their way to unprecedented heights.

There was a workshop I helped run in which we did the most interesting exercise: we had to come up with the worst possible idea imaginable. This comes easier to some than others! The context of the particular challenge was a shopper/marketer one, and this was mine: We're going to hire and train a full-time staff of recipe, nutritional, and product experts who will be permanently stationed in every single supermarket nationwide, at the shelves, by our products. I don't have to explain why this idea stinks, and is a practical impossibility.

The real magic happened next when we had to pivot the idea or figure out if there was an efficient way to make it work. It didn't take much effort or time at all to realize how game-changing it could be with the utilization of FaceTime, WhatsApp, or Skype to facilitate personal (intimate) conversations with shoppers via a remote call center...live! Naturally, the company in question never moved on this idea, but I'm hoping you'll steal it.

An internal kickstarter-esque microfinancing option should be open to all employees for their own participation and investment. After all, why shouldn't employees help fellow employees, and ultimately share in the potential riches?

Smart corporations could match employee contributions or at least determine specific thresholds or milestones, after which the company should back the efforts substantially and ensure they see the light of the day.

I wouldn't stop there. I would extend the opportunity to "friends and family" outside the organization. Think about it: flows of capital coming into the organization, as opposed to just going out.

2. CREATE STICKY SITUATIONS THAT EARN LOYALTY

Holding on to talent is almost an impossibility for large corporations at an entry, junior, or even mid-level tier. Younger-skewing worker bees just don't have the patience to stick around for that special moment when their incompetence is rewarded with a golden parachute (just like the CEO).

Seventy-four percent of millennials who like their jobs are planning to leave within the next three years, according to a study from Qualtrics in 2017. In case you missed it, these are the ones who LIKE their jobs!

I believe it's time to create incentives to stay using the same methodology employed by startups themselves: equity, options, and the ability to vest based upon term (time), milestones (goals), and "events" (transactions).

To be clear, I'm not referring to stock in the company itself (remember, most of these folk are not planning on sticking around long enough anyway). What I'm referring to is equity in their own ideas and ventures. Or equity in the startups they bring into the company and end up working with (as opposed to for.)

For your intrapreneurs, this is like having your cake and eating it, as well. It is the ability to share in the upside of entrepreneurial pursuits without sacrificing the stability and security of a full-time paying job.

Incentivization and compensation are, without question, the one (or two) most important issues associated with talent. In a world becoming ever more commoditized, and where creativity and originality are in such short supply, extracting game-changing contributions from both external partners (digital disruption) and internal stakeholders (winning the talent war) is paramount.

If the shortest distance between two points is a straight line, we now have a clear one that links these two critical pieces of the puzzle.

What kind of message do we send out when we don't share the wealth with the creators? What could possibly motivate your talent to give you their best ideas when they don't stand to benefit from them?

Equity-based or royalty-based compensation is the only viable path forward. Without it, you should always worry if you are suffering from EHB (employees hold back) syndrome.

3. SHARKS, WHALES, AND DOLPHINS

A natural extension or variation of the employee-funding concept is the creation of a specific budget or amount of money that partly or wholly funds employee ideas, which, in turn, directly or indirectly benefit the corporation. While the first two ideas support both original ideas inside and existing ideas outside the company with rewards in the form of equity, this is all about recognizing and elevating status within the company.

The made-for-TV branded approach of Shark Tank (or its global equivalents) has created a perfect proving ground for venture capital and angel investing. If imitation is the sincerest form of flattery, I would advocate copying this model blow for blow, and repurposing it inside your organization. Don't worry, Daymond, I'm sure they'll hire you to keynote and MC the event! You'll probably want to avoid getting the legal eagles too excited by copying the name, so create your own version: Colgate Capitalists, Samsung Speculators, or how about Philips Philanthropists?

4. IF YOU CAN'T BEAT 'EM, HIRE 'EM

The term "acquihire" first circulated around 2005, and the date is not insignificant. It corresponds with a time and place (Silicon Valley) where top engineering talent was so scarce and hard to come by, it made more financial sense to buy a company—even at a premium—and then essentially discard all the technology (thereby placing a value of zero on the app/platform/code), than it did to utilize executive recruiters to find the same talent elsewhere.

The obvious tech giants such as Google, Facebook, and Twitter all partake in this practice, and while you might think of it as indulgent, in reality, it is soundly pragmatic.[3]

Furthermore, large brands are getting in on the act, as well.

When Under Armor acquired MapMyFitness in 2013 for $150 million, what caught my eye was that MapMyFitness founder Robin Thurston became the chief digital officer of Under Armor. Sure, he left 2 ½ years later (July 2016), but in terms of entrepreneurs working for corporates, that's like the dog-years equivalent of two lifetimes. It struck me that more companies should look toward the acquihire as a means of accelerating their digital and innovation roadmaps.

Art imitates life in HBO's hit show *Silicon Valley,* in which Pied Piper reaches out to Optimoji in order to fast-track their developer needs with an acquihire.

5. GAMIFICATION OF EDUCATION

The constant and endless cycle of corporate budget cuts, reorgs, and restructures make progress and momentum inside a company unrealistic.

Earlier, I reflected on something that is tantamount to neglect: when companies expect their "centers of excellence" specialists or subject-matter experts to pay their own way to events like SxSW—but what if we could combine these two "negatives" to make a net positive?

What if training and development were incentivized or gamified? A couple of years ago, I put together a process designed to make learning fun for employees. Instead of boring "lessons" on theory or history of business fundamentals or even tactics associated with emerging platforms, I constructed a framework that would be more of a treasure hunt than a course map, with incentives such as all-expenses-paid trips to festivals like the Consumer Electronics Show (CES) in Vegas, Mobile World Congress in Barcelona, or even Cannes in Nice.

Instead of PowerPoint presentations, there would be challenges such as get @richardbranson to retweet you. Instead of just reading Startup Nation, learners who scored highest on a quiz would get to go to lunch with the authors of the book. Instead of learning the difference between a nervous tick and a live, streaming platform used predominantly for gaming, why not get participants to set up their own Twitch channel for Fortnite to see who could get to 100 streaming subscribers first?

6. ACCELERATE PEOPLE INTO POSITIONS OF LEADERSHIP

There's no point in setting sail to the future if you can't staff your ship with a crack crew, right?

The lack of diversity in business right now is disgraceful.

Hiring is one thing; filling quotas is another. The REAL test, however, is the challenge to identify and ultimately fast-track rising stars within this talent pool—and yes, this includes white guys, albeit young ones.

The Futures program at Mondelēz was specifically designed to excavate young stars and then elevate them within the organization. Part of the "prize" of hand-raisers who volunteered to participate in the program and collaborate with startups was the ability to be positioned as an internal rock star. They got to see their names in lights and their faces across posters, inside and outside their companies. They also got coveted face time with their chief marketing officer, who ordinarily would not have known their name from Adam—unless, of course, their name was Adam, in which case they probably would still have gotten it wrong.

It's a double-edged sword, without question. Creating external visibility is important for your rising stars' egos, but it also puts out a come-and-get-me bat-sign to all worthy suitors. The 40 under 40, 30 under 30, 20 under 20 (and I hear rumors they're starting a 10 under 10) lists are ticking time bombs for the headhunter onslaught, but I would argue that the best anecdote to this scenario is to embrace it head on. Accept it as fact. If your starting point is that you're fighting a losing battle to hold onto talent (and you will lose it), then at least you can take direct steps to be granted a stay of execution. Delaying the inevitable gives you more time to figure out a way to recognize (incentivize) and reward (compensate) them accordingly.

I really like the idea of equity as the new bonus structure (#2 sticky situations), so why not stagger this across multiple years with the same kind of vesting and options plan they would get if they were to join a startup?

Whether granting them equity in external ventures they helped make happen, or in their own ideas that were incubated and funded from within, they now have a real, tangible reason to stick around and make their mark inside the company. The upside is theoretically limitless, and it is something they can influence and impact. This offers a powerful 1-2 punch and allows everyone to win.

It is the best of both worlds.

CHAPTER 11

CUSTOMER OBSESSION

I must confess—I am obsessed. I am obsessed with customers. And you should be too. Your survival depends on it.

The addiction to retention began with my second book, *Join the Conversation*. At that time, everyone and their grandmother wanted to jump on the social-media bandwagon. Companies were falling over one another to take advantage of this new fad. I simply asked, "With whom?" With whom do you wish to join the conversation?" The answer was obvious: your customer!

I was hooked. Drunk on loyalty. I couldn't get enough of my fixation, and so I wrote an entire book called *Flip the Funnel* to show how advocacy could grow a business from the inside out, and how retention could become the new acquisition.

I continued the customer fetish with *Z.E.R.O.*—most notably the "Z" (zealots) and "R" (retention) of Z.E.R.O.

And I'm not done espousing my passion for customer-centricity as the one and only way you can keep your head above the turbulent waters of change and disruption.

So why the continued focus on the whole customer experience thing? I'll give you three primary reasons:

1.   You *still* don't get it.

2.   You really need to get it.

3.   If you get it, you will win. If you don't, you will lose. Very binary.

YOU STILL DON'T GET IT...AND I CAN PROVE IT.

As long as you continue to overspend on "strangers" (first-time buyers) and "prostitutes" (promiscuous switchers) instead of your returning, recurring loyalists or even zealots, you will continue to perpetuate a road to nowhere: the leaky bucket (as you gain new customers, you lose others) or chasm scenario (disproportionate spend relative to revenue contribution).

You'll justify your unhealthy fixation on a bunch of made-up or nonsensical excuses. I once spoke at an event, and an executive from American Express literally justified their fixation on acquisition based upon the fact that their customer base was too old and literally dying on them.

Er, don't you think customers should be dying to get in...versus dying to get out?

Look, I've been asked every question under the sun about this:

- **Does it work as well for B2B as it does for B2C?** Yes, it does. Even more so, actually.

- **Does it work as well for small and medium-sized businesses as it does for big business?** Yes, it does. Even more so, actually.

- **Is it worth it? Let me work it, I put my thing down, flip it and reverse it:**[1] It costs less to acquire a new customer via an existing one than it does to acquire one using traditional means. When retention becomes the new acquisition, you can build a business from the inside out.

- **What about a new company like a startup, or an existing company looking to launch a new service line or product?** YES, IT DOES. As long as you have one single customer, you can "use existing customers to gain new ones." You also have a mother, and everyone's mother will gladly be your first customer and tell her bridge club or send her plastic-surgery support group a WhatsApp. In addition, your "first customers" are extremely special. Don't forget this, or forget them. I call this the "first customer theory."

THIS ONE IS NOT OPTIONAL

As I will touch upon later, I don't believe every company has to be best-in-class in all four pillars in order to have an elevated chance of survival. It's also possible to deliver on three of the four pillars; for example, without meaningful adverse consequences. I will say, however, that this one is absolutely mandatory. It is absolutely vital to deliver sufficiently on customer obsession. This one cannot fall through the cracks.

Companies that have found success—and, by definition, sucked less—have done so with an acute focus on customer-centricity, or customer obsession.

Take Netflix. If you want the reason why they shut down their DVD service the day they shipped their billionth DVD, perhaps the answer lies in the fact they just followed their customer to the hallowed hills of streaming. Instead of listening to Wall Street analysts or those obsessed with the bottom line, they focused on a different obsession.

Disrupting Blockbuster by eliminating late fees was just the start. In fact, it was too easy. Instead of disintermediating them, they went for something a lot more fatal: discombobulating them. Disintegrating them. Destroying them by recognizing that there were still too many points of friction associated with putting a DVD into a sleeve and dropping said sleeve into the mail. Perhaps Reed Hastings was truly one step ahead, and recognized the rise of streaming and/or the fall of snail mail. Or perhaps he just heard what his customers were saying...or weren't saying. Perhaps he was just looking to make it as easy as humanly possible to be able to "rent" a movie in the short term or near future.

According to Joris Evers, Director of Global Communications at Netflix, "There are 33 million different versions of Netflix." That's not just PR spin. It's kind of true. Seventy-five percent of Netflix viewer activity is based upon recommendations, but where do these recommendations come from? They come from an AI, a big-data-infused personalization engine built on customer obsession.

Things like when you pause, rewind, or fast forward...the date you watch...what time you watch content...where you watch (zip code)...which device you use to watch...when you pause and leave content (and if you ever come back)...the ratings given (about 4 million per day)...searches (about 3 million per day)...browsing and scrolling behavior...data within movies—all of this informs your recommendations.

Actually, Netflix takes this one step further, and uses the actual searches to brief, commission, and ultimately execute entire original series.

In 2011, Netflix made one of the biggest decisions they'll ever make: they outbid the likes of HBO and AMC for *House of Cards*[2]. Their $100 million gamble was a calculated one, as they crunched and triangulated real audience viewership data and incorporated items like:

- Complete views of the David Fincher-directed movie *The Social Network* from start to finish

- Viewership of The British version of *House of Cards*

- Overlap of the above with Kevin Spacey (obviously criminal background check was not a part of this process) films, and/or films directed by David Fincher.

When you can build a recommendation engine that is truly customer-obsessed (like Amazon), there is only one likely outcome: world domination at the expense of the also-rans—the poor schlubs who are prisoners to special interests, self-interest, legacy partnerships, union demands, and the like.

THERE IS NO *A* OR *I* IN CUSTOMER, BUT THERE SHOULD BE

Artificial intelligence is really one of the most poorly understood and poorly applied phenomena. I blame IBM and Watson for prematurely hyping nothing more than a glorified weather forecast or Trivial Pursuit (Jeopardy) champion. Perhaps what we need is a really compelling use case, or maybe we just need a better strategic framework.

I came up with this one: automation – augmentation – auguration as a crawl-walk-run approach. Would it surprise you to learn that we're still very early on in this continuum? We're still referring to replacing human tasks with machines as Artificial Intelligence. It's neither artificial nor intelligent, but it does put plenty of people out of work on the road to improving the bottom line! Pat yourselves on the back, bloodsuckers!

In addition, I would have you rethink AI from a purely customer-centric lens. Using my continuum, this is how it would look:

Automation: Machine-led menial tasks to save customers time and money and make their lives easier

Augmentation: Humans and machines working hand in hand to offer a better overall customer experience to make their lives better

Auguration: Machine-led magic to surprise and delight customers by anticipating their next moves, fixing problems before they begin, or simply presenting a sublime recommendation, customization, or personalization customer cocktail to make their lives richer

AI is, without question, the mystery basket ingredient in the *Chopped* version of business. Forget to use it in your recipe, and you're instantly disqualified. Use it well, and you are well on your way to becoming *Chopped* champion and earning your Michelin star.

AI will be both pervasive and ubiquitous in each facet of every business's process, supply chain, value chain, and customer journey. Which is precisely why large companies are doomed to fail. Their legacy partnerships and systems are just not set up to integrate or upgrade with new technologies in general, or with AI specifically. The larger the system, the harder it is to shift away from it.

It's not that they don't want to change; it's just that they can't!

"It's not that large corporations don't want to change; it's just that they can't!"

As long as big business continues to sign ginormous legacy deals with similar large tech vendors as part of a like-for-like deal that centers around scale, the price to pay will be one of inevitable demise.

Unfortunately, this scenario is less a win-win and more a zero-sum exercise in futility, in which only one side is benefiting longer-term; and it's not the buyer! My warning to you is clear: get out of these deals any way you can, or, at a minimum, institute one-year renegotiation—or even cancelation—clauses.

Negotiating Hail Mary clauses into all future (and hopefully existing legacy) partner contracts that allow shorter-term renegotiation intervals would give corporations a fighting chance at staying in the game. Five-year+ terms are tantamount to death sentences, especially when new actors become hostage to deals—which are often products of nepotism, kickbacks, double-dipping from ruthless salespeople, or short-sighted finance and procurement number-crunchers.

Blow up the whole miserable lot, or risk going down with the ship.

CONFUCIUS MAY BE CONFUSED, BUT YOUR CUSTOMER SHOULDN'T BE

Early on in my career, I learned one universal truth: follow the consumer. She will never lie. Listen to your customer. He speaks the truth (even when he is wrong). Technically, that might be 1½ truths, but either way, it's a universal truth, and a North Star that should govern everything you are and everything you do. Your marketing function plays—or should play—a critical role in being able to deliver (and hopefully over-deliver) against this mandate. Whether you call it customer service, relationship marketing, or customer-relationship marketing (CRM); whether you approach it with a distinctly "analog" or "manual" human touch, or go completely machine-powered, you need to pay attention, or you will surely pay a price that you just cannot afford to pony up.

As long as your sherpa is your consumer, you never will be led astray. Your consumers leave trails behind them. Engagement slime. Data breadcrumbs. Sometimes, it's subtle. Other times, it's kick-in-the nuts obvious. In the case of the Kmart example mentioned earlier in the book, consider three things:

1. There may not have been "critical mass" in terms of the number of Kmart customers online at the time, or those accessing the likes of AOL using broadband connections. The key phrase is "at the time," because every single key indicator was moving in the right direction. For what it's worth, we've known this since 1965, when Moore's Law was published. That was the first hint that things were about to go "ludicrous speed," and so the real issue is less about if we are on the right track, and more about whether or not we can keep up!

2. Had Kmart implemented this idea back then, it could very well have become a revenue generator—possibly a spinoff business. Who knows, perhaps Kmart and Pearson Education could have merged early on. Two legacy businesses for the price of one.

3. Most importantly, had they done this back in 2001, they might have escaped scraping the bottom of the deep-discount barrel and playing catch-up with Walmart, and instead leapfrogged over Sears instead of being attached to them.

The real issue is less about if we are on the right track, and more about whether or not we can keep up!

Don't be like Kmart. Or most companies that are often gifted with what equates to a game-changing opportunity, only to miss out for reasons that were well within their control. Think about how far you could have come had you just pulled the trigger versus being trapped in the quicksand of procrastination, politics, and red tape!

Timing is Everything

Walmart purchased Jet.com, but did you know they had a chance to purchase Amazon.com? I had heard rumors of this, and so when in doubt, I turned to the crowd, specifically Quora. Within hours of asking the question, "Is it true that Walmart had a chance to buy Amazon?" I received this response from CJ Lu Sing, writer at *The Boring Blog.*

This answer takes its evidence from *The Everything Store,* a biography on Jeff Bezos and Amazon written by Brad Stone. According to Stone's writing, early in the Age of Amazon, Jeff Bezos and other Amazon executives met with Walmart higher-ups. It was a brief meeting. The meeting was conducted in secret, and apparently is now regarded as nothing more than a footnote in history. The meeting didn't go very far, and Jeff Bezos was adamant about remaining independent from the behemoth retailer. We will never know if Walmart was serious about acquiring Amazon, or if they even offered a legitimate deal to Amazon's executives.

It's pretty commonplace to find venture arms within large corporations, but in almost all cases, I have been uniformly disappointed with the lack of vision, the quality of the offerings, and the approach to acquisitions. It's not necessarily the caliber of the people running these funds, nor is it about their qualifications; rather, it is about their mandate (which is often out of their control.) They are typically investment bankers, VCs, or collateral damage from yet another internal reorg (non-venture people being thrust into a role for which they have limited experience or expertise).

What is often absent and sorely lacking is the marketing skillset—specifically, the ability to imagine a better future for their company—and a bolder, consumer-led reality and brighter financial outcome for their shareholders.

SPEED TO MARKET IS DIRECTLY CORRELATED WITH A SUPERIOR CUSTOMER EXPERIENCE

In *Flip the Funnel,* my mind was blown when Dustin Curtis took the liberty of redesigning American Airlines' website and equating a bad website and user experience with customer experience: "If I was running a company with the distinction and history of American Airlines, I would be embarrassed—no, ashamed—to have a website with a customer experience as terrible as the one you have now...."

Speed to market, or really just the ability to move more quickly, is a hallmark of the startup, but both are foreign bodies when it comes to big business. It is another nail in the coffin of the corporation that is built to slow, and thus built to suck.

It can take as long as 18 months for a pair of shoes to go from a designer's sketchpad to a retailer's register. But now, Betabrand is doing it in only five days... and it aims to make the process even faster through a sublime combination of crowdsourcing and 3D digital rendering.

By bringing consumers into the product-development ecosystem, Betabrand is able to compress the timeline for designers, merchants, and marketers to identify design tastes. By putting these prototypes on presale, they can determine how large a given production run should be.

No more guesswork. No more waste on the supply side.

Delighted customers with skin in the game on the demand side.

It still takes four months to fulfill the orders, but customers don't mind when they have a vested interest in the products themselves. The 30 percent discount for pre-orders doesn't hurt, either!

Figure 11.1 - Closing the Loop

5 WAYS TO MAKE YOUR OBSESSION TANGIBLE

1. Customer of the Month

We celebrate our top employees with Employee of the Month awards; we even display their photos for all our customers to see on the walls of our offices, stores, and showrooms. So why not reverse the roles? Recognizing a Customer of the Month works unbelievably well within the business-to-business environment, in particular—especially when showcasing the individual and their capabilities can lead to future connections and engagements to grow their business. Becoming a true connector and enabler on behalf of clients can take the value of a company to a whole new level, and, in doing so, create elevated preference and loyalty.

2. Customer Funerals

On the flipside is the idea of mourning every lost customer as a loss. This means, quite literally, to put on a funeral for the customer. Wear black. Shed some tears (even crocodile ones). Tear your clothing. Hold a wake. Above all, recite a eulogy for the dearly departed. Instead of accepting their departure as an acceptable loss within a statistically-significant margin of error—in other words, looking at them merely as an attrition number—I want you to obsess about every aspect of their humanity.

Who were they? Why did they choose to give you their business in the first place? Why did they leave? What could you have done differently? What could you have done better? Could you have seen the signs earlier? Why not conduct exit interviews for all of your customer exits? Don't have the people power? Too bad. Get some of those fat cats in the boardroom to get off their lazy asses and do some real work for a change.

3. Priceless Experiences

Companies today are built to suck, because they refuse to acknowledge that they are just overpriced commodities. This sham is magnified when existing customers are mistreated, abused, neglected, and deprioritized in favor of the aforementioned strangers and prostitutes. Instead of punishing them by offering promotions, discounts, or deals to first-time customers only, why not reward them for their tenure with priceless experiences?

So what is a priceless experience? I describe it as something money can't buy— or, even if it could, the perceived value is so much higher. Mastercard may very well share my view on this (don't sue!).

Blue Board describes themselves as experiential employee rewards for the modern workplace. Instead of offering up small cash bonuses, gift cards, certificates of appreciation, or even that retirement Rolex, Blue Board brings incentives and rewards that include the likes of The James Bond Experience, Intro to Flying Trapeze, Feed Sharks at the Aquarium, The Art of Standup Comedy, and Zero-Gravity Float Therapy.

Feel free to add this idea to the talent resurrection section from earlier in the book as idea number 7, but why stop with your employees? Surely, this makes as much sense for customers, as well?

I had the pleasure of spending some time with the Mets organization a few years back. I offered up the following idea to them: what if you could reward every season ticketholder on their 20-year anniversary with the ability to sit in the dugout with the manager for an inning?

The way to position and ultimately sell it is through simple math—not myth. Each Major League Baseball team plays 81 home games every season. How many fans do you think would be celebrating their 20-year season ticket anniversary every year? 81? More? Less? Does it seem like a lot to have one customer per game sit all googly-eyed for one inning? And if that number scares the daylights out of you (unless it's a night game), increase the anniversary term to 25 years. That number would drop exponentially. I get the seriousness and intensity of a competitive game, but if a manager can put on a headset and offer up television interviews in the middle of a game, surely he can handle the distraction of a customer who has given them consistent business for over

20 years? Perhaps if we assigned a dollar value to this equation, it would make it even more appealing. For starters, I'm assuming most people buy 2 or more season tickets, so we can double or even treble the ticket revenue. Now factor in all the overpriced peanuts and crackerjacks, popcorn, corn dogs, and beer, coupled with all the jerseys, spirit gear, accessories, and memorabilia. It's a ton of money in exchange for one inning and a life-changing experience.

I cheated on my beloved English Football Club, Tottenham Hotspur, by purchasing a season ticket to Major League Soccer's New York City F.C. (it was research, I swear!). I was pretty impressed with the various ways they handled advocacy, and specifically how I could exchange my loyalty points for priceless experiences. During my time as a customer, my son got to walk onto the field with a player, we got to watch the player warm-ups, and my boys will never forget the meet-and-greet with the players after a match (which, fortunately, they won).

Figure 11.2 - Jack and NYCFC

I actually think this idea is as much an acquisition idea as it is a retention one. Think about it. Would you commit to purchasing a season ticket today if you knew in 20 years' time, you'd get to sit in the dugout with the manager or have the players dump a barrel of Gatorade on you at the end of the match as their MVP?

You don't need to answer. It's obvious.

4. Put the Custom in Customer

A large company is designed around repeatable, scalable processes. It's a one-size-fits-all approach that some might call standardization, but I would call it a fast-track to "commoditization," especially when we start hearing things like, "If we make an exception for you, we'll have to make an exception for all of our customers!" Remember the 33 million versions of Netflix? The only "sameness" should be the unifying vision around customer obsession and treating each customer uniquely—and yes, even differently.

The difficulty of meeting this challenge really epitomizes how the economies of scale that once were responsible for the growth, profitability, and competitive advantage of the corporation are now the exact cause of its demise. Repeatable processes just become straw after straw on that poor camel's back!

Amazon became the second trillion-dollar company in 2018, joining Apple. As an aside, I figured we needed a name for a trillion-dollar company, given that billion-dollar companies are called unicorns. I'm oscillating between Phoenix and Hydra, depending on whether you are on the giving or receiving end. I think I'd go with Phoenix due to its symbolism of eternal life, but the reality is that even the phoenix's life comes to an end (about once in a thousand years). No company is immortal, as you'll see later in the book. Legend has it that only one can exist at a time, and that may also be true, as Apple has been bibbing and bobbing in and out of Phoenix territory. The jury may be out on what to call a trillion-dollar company, but there's no doubt about the name for most large companies that are built to suck: the Dodo!

Going back to the idea of standardization versus customization, just look at how Amazon personalizes their entire service-suite down to the granular site and recommendation level. A Harvard Business Review paper[3] on the strategic intent of companies identifies three distinct approaches: operational excellence, customer intimacy, and product leadership.

What should jump out at you is the overreliance of large companies on operational excellence—scale begets cost savings—as opposed to the other two categories.

It is possible to create enterprise-ready customer obsession engines.

Footcare brand Dr. Scholl's created in-store kiosks which guide the consumer toward making a purchase decision based upon foot measurements that can be taken right in-store to deliver customized orthotics, whereas Walmart created a mechanism for consumers to walk directly into a store and purchase prescription eyeglasses based upon a "self-diagnosis."

No one said this was going to be easy, but it's mission-critical that you figure out how to be all things to all people all the time. Or else.

5. Get out of Jail Free

It wouldn't be a Jaffe book without an airline story, and for this, I will, as always, defer to my one true love: American Airlines. In 2017, I had my first light-flying year since 2005. For the first time in 12 years, I flew less than 100,000 miles on American, and as a result, I missed qualifying for Executive Platinum (or Emerald One World) status. I was mortified.

So I called American and told them my sob story. They were intrigued, and offered to investigate. Time passed. I got restless, turned to the inner OCD frequent traveler in me, and tweeted United, Delta, or anyone who would listen asking for a "status match." To their credit, United Airlines was the only one to respond, though they didn't automatically match my status (if they had, the story would end here.)

Instead, they offered me a status challenge: if I flew a certain number of miles over a three-month period, I would receive their highest tier. Unfortunately (for them), this did not include their alliance partners, and with a ticket already booked to South Africa on South African Airlines, I could not move forward.

Next up was Delta, who subsequently rejected the match, as apparently I had mindlessly accepted a free upgrade to their lowest tier (Silver) several years back. For my troubles, they also sent my luggage to Amsterdam instead of Cape Town for six long days.

I returned to American and waited. And waited. After two more internal reviews, I received special dispensation to complete the Executive Platinum challenge, which, incredibly, was not open to me right off the bat. I had to plead and essentially make my case as to why I "deserved" the chance to maintain my status for one more year. I don't want to sound ungrateful, but why on earth does the onus fall on me (the customer) to advocate on my own behalf? As a 2,000,000-miler and an Executive Platinum member for 12 years, surely I should have been given the benefit of the doubt.

Here's an idea I call Get out of Jail Free, which is a hat tip to the popular board game Monopoly. When you have one of these cards, you get a chance to play it if you are sent to jail, and, like the name suggests, get out of it. Free. Profound, I know.

It's similar to gamifying customer experience with priceless rewards. Why not offer up tenure-based mulligans to customers who have had a bad day? Here are some examples:

- For a customer who misses qualifying for a premium loyalty tier (me), offer them a "card" for every 10 consecutive years they've qualified to exchange for guaranteed status.

- In the financial services sector, instead of spiking a customer's APR on a late credit card payment, maintain their low rate for every 5 years of on-time payments.

- In the insurance space, offer incentives for good driving records (this is already being done!)

By the way, I easily requalified for Executive Platinum for the 2019 calendar year, and estimate that both Delta and United lost out on roughly $50,000 in revenue from me in the process.

So, what should you take away from this?

There's no happy ending, and no real winner. American retained my business, but only because their competitors were too shortsighted and narrow-minded. By simply paying attention and using the smallest amount of common sense, they could have offered an automatic status match for one year. Had they done that, I would have left American, and would have been all theirs! Twelve+ years of loyalty and positive experiences would have been eviscerated by one act of humanity from a customer-obsessed competitor.

Obsession is typically considered to be unhealthy. Like boiling the rabbit of your jilted lover. In this case, however, it is a very necessary means to an extremely healthy outcome: survival...and even thrival.

CHAPTER 12

CORPORATE CITIZENSHIP

Hugh Evans is a visionary. Hugh Evans is an entrepreneur. Hugh Evans is a humanitarian. Hugh Evans is an Aussie. Three out of four isn't too bad, is it?

In 2008, he founded the Global Poverty Project with a $60,000 USD grant from the United Nations, a $350,000 AUD grant from AusAID, and a delusional goal of making poverty history by 2030. I was introduced to Hugh by my "brother from another mother," Clive Burcham. Clive is another Aussie who believes passionately in the combined power of creativity, responsibility, and purpose to remake the world into a better place.

Hugh's model is sublime. He built a robust activism engine utilizing high-value actions by citizens, from content-sharing to retweeting to signing a petition to calling your local senator. These were incentivized with (priceless) rewards and headlined by an annual mega-festival concert in New York's Central Park as well as several tentpole events around the globe. Want a ticket to go to the Mandela 100 Global Citizen Festival in Johannesburg and see Beyonce, Jay-Z, Usher, and Ed Sheeran, to name a few? You can buy them, but if you want them for free, you can earn them through the aforementioned high-value actions. This is gamifying activism!

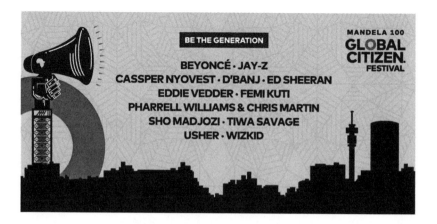

Figure 12.1 - Global Citizen Festival

Hugh and the Global Poverty Project don't talk business. They mean business. They demonstrate their intent, ambition, and intensity through action instead of rhetoric.

It was this inspiration that helped me form the fourth and final pillar of the survival table: the notion that corporations (if they have any chance of avoiding inevitable extinction) have to become global citizens themselves to live this promise and potential to the max...each and every day of their lives.

Of course, the concept of global citizenship is not necessarily a new one. Wikipedia has this to say: *Global citizenship is the idea of all persons having rights and civic responsibilities that come with being a member of the world with whole-world philosophy and sensibilities, rather than a citizen of a particular nation or place. The idea is that one's identity transcends geography or political borders, and that responsibilities or rights are derived from membership in a broader class: humanity.*

There's a lot to unpack in this very small blurb, but I think it speaks strongly to the idea that corporations not only have a responsibility to step up and own up to a higher calling and challenge, but indeed, that this move can, and most likely will, prove to be their salvation.

I think there is particular significance in this definition. Industry bigwigs tout companies as brands with human qualities. If that is the case, what better way to demonstrate this humanity than by displaying human traits like empathy, kindness, generosity, and selflessness to make a tangible difference in the world? A new take on capitalism: be good to others, and they will do good in return! Whole Foods founder John Mackey calls this Conscious Capitalism, and even wrote a book on it.

To come up with a good name for this category, I flirted between global corporate citizenship and corporate global citizenship, but decided to drop the word global. Here's why: large corporations are, by nature, global in both physical and digital footprint and capabilities. Surely, their resultant commitment should reflect this broad brush? "Think global, act local" is a popular aphorism in business, but today, "think local, act global" might be a better way to reframe the idea of making a difference...at scale.

This might sound trite, but in order to do good, you first have to be good. That's where all of this goes to hell in a handbasket. Most corporations couldn't give a continental hoot about making the world a better place. It's a tax deduction; a necessary evil; a watchdog line item on a superficial checklist.

BUSINESS SHOULD HAVE A CONSCIENCE

Ex-Unilever CMO Keith Weed was quoted at an Interactive Advertising Bureau conference as saying, *"Fake news, racism, sexism, terrorists spreading messages of hate, toxic content directed at children...it is in the digital media industry's interest to listen and act on this. Before viewers stop viewing, advertisers stop advertising, and publishers stop publishing."*

Stands like this are common in the marketplace. Chief executives and their officers are only too familiar when it comes to grabbing headlines with sensational comments of emptiness. What made *this* a little meatier, though, was the fact that Unilever threatened to pull all of their advertising from the offending culprits—led by Facebook and Google—unless they took significant steps to clean up their acts.

Last year, Unilever spent $9.4 billion on marketing, and about a third of that on digital advertising, making it one of the medium's biggest advertisers. So they have a pretty influential voice. Facebook and Google alone take in 60 percent of all digital advertising. So it is in their best interest to listen. Intently.

BEER TODAY, GONE TOMORROW

It's no secret that iconic brands like Budweiser are struggling nowadays to stem the continuous erosion in their market share, thanks to a multitude of imported and craft beers—plus everything from the resurgence of rosé to the popularity of Aperol Spritz to the inexorable rise of premium tequila. The open-collared shirts at AB InBev are racking their brains to reverse the curse, but unfortunately, all they seem to come up with is new advertising campaigns or taglines. They even changed the name of their iconic beer to America during the Summer of 2016 to ~~protest~~ remind people they were as familiar as blue jeans or apple pie. I guess familiarity breeds contempt!

Enter the violin strings of corporate social responsibility meets public relations! During the Super Bowl of 2018, they spent about $5,000,000 in media, and who knows how much in agency and production fees on at least one 30-second commercial to tell us all how awesome they are. According to an Anheuser-Busch press release, they delivered over 2 million cans of water to communities hit by hurricanes, flooding, or wildfires over the course of 2017.

I wondered how many additional cans of water they could have sent to ailing communities had they not attempted to advertise their self-servicing magnanimity. Perhaps they should have watched Schindler's List one more time before making this decision. Or consulted with their bottling bedfellow, PepsiCo, to get a proper debrief on what happens when you mix activism and commercialism (just ask Kendall Jenner).

To be clear and fair, AB InBev deserves credit (likewise with Gillette's 2019 Super Bowl effort to donate one million dollars to help men be less clueless) for everything they did...and there are scores of companies who do significantly less, if anything at all. Perhaps a corporation *should* have to spend their media dollars to demonstrate their commitment to set an example for other companies to follow suit.

In *Join the Conversation,* I said, "Marketing is not a campaign; it's a commitment." The commitment in question alluded to the rise of social media as a means of introducing a powerful R.E.A.C.H. (which stands for Responsive, Empathetic, Accessible, Connected, and Human) component to the existing customer relationship. Some years later, I expanded on this thinking: from campaigns to commitments to ecosystems, a people-centric ecosystem powered by technology that connects the dots between customers and customers, employees and employees, and employees and customers.

It's now time to introduce the next evolution of this journey: from campaigns to commitments to ecosystems to movements. Let me ask you this: where do your corporate social responsibility efforts lie? Are they prostrated on an Excel spreadsheet like a media flowchart? Or are they part of your cultural core, on a par with (or elevated beyond) the prime directive of increasing shareholder value above all else?

In a particular episode of my favorite marketing podcast, The Beancast (I am a regular guest on the panel), the guests discussed various brands' misguided efforts and even failed attempts at ingratiating themselves during Women's Day. In particular, they discussed McDonald's turning their iconic Golden Arches—the M—upside-down to reveal....tada...a W. As in W for women... hear them roar! To really bring home their altruistic commitment, they advertised the heck out of it and even paid USD $2,000,000 to physically turn some of their arches around—stopping short, of course, of changing their name to WcDonald's to pay tribute to the fairer sex.[1]

Figure 12.1 - WcDonald's

For all their gallant efforts, the hashtag #droopyboobs started trending to reward them for all their efforts!

To quote panelist Saul Colt on the show: *"I hate to single out McDonald's, but here's where they and all the brands were really short-sighted with International Women's Day. It was the transactional nature of the stunts. They did nothing but invite criticism. So if you know people are going to complain anyway, why not do something amazing for them to complain about that has a lasting effect?*

Now, I read the McDonald's stunt cost $2 million. They flipped a couple of signs. Most of the flipping of signs was really just done digitally, but there were a handful of stores where they gave them new uniforms. They went all out, and did the whole stunt. $2 million. Now, imagine if they gave that $2 million—this is what I would have done—to Planned Parenthood. Do something that would actually *have a lasting effect. People are still going to complain. People are still going to talk about it. People are going to still—you're going to alienate half of your audience no matter what. But think about that. Who's going to really, really, really complain wholeheartedly about a donation that goes directly to women, that is going to give specific attention, needed just for women? We're talking about International Women's Day. So it's crazy. What they should have done is, instead of flip a couple signs, they should have paid for a hundred pap smears and mammograms."*

I think this is a fantastic point, and I also loved this quote from another panelist on the same show: "You think that people would notice that we didn't do this yesterday and we are not going to do it tomorrow," which sounds so obvious, but makes the point beautifully that being a corporate citizen has to be something that is inextricably part of a company's DNA and reason for being.

I want to make another point about being a corporate citizen and built to serve instead of a corporate marauder that is built to blow (hot air, rhetoric, empty promises), and I'll use the alcohol industry once again.

Companies in the alcoholic beverage category all follow the same corporate-social-responsibility playbook guidelines to "drink responsibly." In most cases, it's tiny print at the bottom of another print ad that represents the standard admissions of lies, untruths, loopholes, and exceptions you see in standard terms and conditions. In some cases, they'll take it up a notch by dedicating an entire creative message to celebrating the designated driver.

So, in the spirit of embracing your heresy, specifically the idea of leaving money on the table, what if an alcohol company explicitly turned their backs on their customers who drink and drive—"firing" them, so to speak—by stating, "We don't want your business; go and buy from our competitor, instead!" They could bring this to life by partnering with another endangered corporate species, like a car company, to manufacture cars with built-in breathalyzers that immobilize the car if the owner is over the limit (fingerprint or FaceID verification could prevent cheating the system.)

An additional partnership with the likes of Uber or Lyft could trigger an automatic call for a ride to bring this baby home...literally. This is the one time I would wholeheartedly advocate for collusion (I'm sure Donald agrees with me), whereby every single one of the alcohol conglomerates could or should join forces with every single one of the automotive manufacturers to do their part to be true corporate citizens.

Of course, there are many less "heretical" solutions, such as building, investment, or buying a breathalyzer app and hoping the customer does the right thing (dream on.) There are also several innovative promotion and distribution strategies that could be deployed, including selling these accessories through liquor stores or even subsidizing them based on actual proof of purchase!

MIRROR AND GLASS: THE STRATEGIC CASE FOR CORPORATE CITIZENSHIP

In the era of built to last, corporations were giant, shiny mirrors offering projections to their constituents, which hopefully were designed to reflect back their own perceptions, expectations, and experiences of doing business with the company. The mirror is indicative of the essence of brands, branding, and brand-building. Focus groups are conducted via one-way mirrors. Brand advertising is essentially a hall of mirrors filled with special effects, bells, and whistles designed to create aspirational magnets of anticipation. When Nike says just do it, you look into the mirror and don't see chubby hubby, but instead the man you could become...if you just...did...it! There's nothing wrong with a reflection, especially if it is indicative of reality or an aspirational and attainable derivative.

The problem however, is that a reflection is not real: Real as in Reality. Not real as in inauthentic. Not real as in smoke and mirrors. Even virtual reality (a brand favorite) might appear to be lifelike, but it isn't alive.

What you see are symbols, images, copy, and moving pictures. Ethereal renderings of people, but not real people.

A reflection represents opacity, not transparency, and the world is moving—quickly—toward complete transparency.

When you go to a fancy restaurant, the trend today is to be able to see the cooks in the kitchen. If you are really important, you might even get seated at the chef's table IN the kitchen.

As indicated earlier, companies are now hostage to Glassdoor, with a direct window into their souls—or at least the souls of disgruntled employees who, more often than not, are emboldened to spill the beans on the bad behavior of the bad actors in their company (even while they're working there).

Need another proof point? Look no further than the #metoo movement, which has torn down the walls that separated the inner sanctum of the corporation and the court of public opinion.

The corporate citizen lives in a glass house, which is one reason why they shouldn't (or wouldn't) throw stones. They are judged by their actions, not by their intent. They are evaluated not by the promises they make, but the promises they keep.

For companies that don't know their purpose (and believe me, there are plenty paying top dollar for this revelation), here's some free advice that will save you a ton of money in the process: like the very transparent nature of glass, go back to a time when you were completely naked. Go back to the beginning. Just like Denny's. If you don't know your purpose, it's only because you've lost your way. Hopefully, you'll find your way home before it's too late...

YOU CAN'T FAKE AUTHENTICITY

If you struggle to find the line between real and fake, I give you this anecdote:

Over the July 4th break (America's Independence Day), Rosey Blair and her boyfriend, Houston Hardaway, were flying from New York to Dallas, but weren't sitting next to each other. They asked a woman sitting next to Houston to swap seats, and she duly obliged. They even made a lighthearted joke that she would end up sitting next to Mr. Right. That's exactly what happened, when Helen and her seatmate, Euan Holden, hit it off. Kind of.

What happened next was indicative of the times we're living in right now. Rosey and her beau live-tweeted (damn you, in-flight WiFi) the entire alleged unfolding romance, using the hashtag #planebae (not to be confused with #saltbae). The whole thing....of course...went viral when the usual suspects (like The Today Show) picked it up.

And you know what's coming next, right? Of course you do! Opportunist corporations just had to get in on the act with their real-time tweetage. No doubt, the junior account people at the advertising agency were doing backflips at what had just dropped onto their tray tables. Alaska Airlines rewarded Rosey with a free flight for her good-Samaritan "good deed," while T-Mobile offered her free WiFi. More like WTFi!

Helen, on the other hand, was not "on board" at all. Instead of riding her newfound fame all the way to the pop-culture bank, Helen promptly withdrew her deposit and closed her account in a tersely-worded statement about "a digital-age cautionary tale about privacy, identity, ethics, and consent." Zing.

Look, there are three sides to every story: yours, mine, and the truth. Truth be told, about ten years ago, I would have been all over this story as testament to the power of social media and what I call "socialdipity" (serendipity in the social age). With that said, I don't think I would have been a booster of the invasion of privacy, or of dumb brands doing dumb marketing. Not every aspect of our Big Brother life has to be beamed or streamed in "real time," or, even worse, commercialized by corporate opportunists.

The Broadway smash hit *Dear Evan Hansen* touches on this all-too-familiar theme. When we signed up for a lifetime subscription of social media, we seemingly *signed away* our rights, decency, shame, and integrity. We received the triple pack of good, bad, and ugly—all rolled into one big hot mess called memes.

Was this a hoax? Maybe. Are Rosey and Houston opportunists? Probably.

Rosey Blair
@roseybeeme

If anyone wants to write a screenplay ... I'm an actress, comedian and a writer and so is my dude. Also if anyone wants to send us plane tickets we are more than happy to try and find your very own #PlaneBae 😍 😌 😂

2:19 PM · Jul 4, 2018

♡ 4,374 ♡ 260 people are talking about this

Figure 12.3 - A Cautionary Tale

Was Helen a little prudish? Ungrateful? Shortsighted? For every person who says yes, there'll be someone who says no.

Perception lives in the eye of the beholder, but in a world of mirrors and glass, *"perception is reality"* has been replaced with *"reality is reality."* This might all sound a little too philosophical, but if you're Alaska Airlines or T-Mobile, don't you feel a little dirty right now with your free Wi-Fi in exchange for loss of privacy? Go take a bath, bro.

Wouldn't we all be better off if we replaced the mirrors of deception (how we want the world to perceive us) with the glass of reality (how we actually are)?

Could you see a scenario in which Alaska Airlines or T-Mobile bans Rosey or Houston from using WiFi in the future, publicly chides them, or secretly offers Helen and Euan a private flight to an undisclosed location in order to pursue their connection the *right way?* Don't hold your breath....

DON'T DO THAT...DO THIS

Companies like Bombas (socks), ThirdLove (bras) or Tom's Shoes (shoes) have built corporate citizenship into their very core. ThirdLove has donated over $3.5 million dollars worth of bras in the past few years to charities around the United States, and they didn't even need a Super Bowl ad to tell the story. They have me!

Companies like these (and if you were paying attention, you'd have noted that these are all newly-formed companies that incorporate direct-to-consumer business models and revenue streams) don't need to convince their share-holders why this makes sense, for two reasons: 1) they don't have shareholders; or 2) their shareholders signed onto this model from the get-go.

For existing or incumbent companies, implementing this kind of go-to-market approach is extremely difficult, if not impossible. This doesn't mean they should all throw in the towel and go home. It just means they have to work that much harder in order to see some signs of life and progress. And, of course, stay the course.

Perhaps it's time for corporations to come clean and admit how hard it is, but at the same time declare unwavering commitment to making the needed changes. Honesty is the best policy, provided it's ultimately backed up, at some point, with action.

THE FORK IN THE ROAD APPLIES EQUALLY TO YOUR CONSUMER

The only North Star of the endangered corporation is bottom line. This is an extremely short-term fixation that is not only short-sighted it's essentially a death warrant.

Think about it from your consumer's standpoint. Who will they ultimately choose to do business with in a world that is becoming increasingly commoditized? Procter & Gamble with their mass-produced feminine hygiene products and their "questionable ingredients?" This was the question posed by Lola, a subscription service delivering tampons and pads, condoms, lubricant, and feminine cleansing wipes. Let's wish them congratulations on closing $24 million in Series B funding in June of 2018.

If it seems like I am being overly harsh on P&G, you're right. They run numerous efforts in Africa to help rehabilitate young women who have been sexually abused or harmed. They have donated canned goods to flood victims in Puerto Rico.

The point I am hammering home is that if this is a deprioritized, tangential, or ancillary part of their business, they will continue to march toward a reality in which they will be OUT of business. The talk must be matched by the walk.

Being a corporate citizen implies living according to an honor code of sorts. Take The We Company, who announced in 2018 that they would no longer reimburse employees for meals that include meat, poultry, or pork, and will stop serving meat at company events.

The We Company's Chief Culture Officer, Miguel McKelvey explained that this was done in order to reduce the company's carbon footprint, and that the policy will save 445.1 million pounds of carbon dioxide emissions by 2023, 16.6 billion gallons of water, and 15,507,103 animals.

It seems the world has gone mad. On the one hand, you have the carnivorous conservatives; and on the other, the herbivore liberals. So where, exactly, should the corporation sit? Feebly take sides (like the Pepsi-Kendell Jenner fiasco or McDonald's and National Women's Day), stay on the fence and take a Swiss approach (those who stand for nothing fall for anything),[2] or take a stand like Nike did when they made Colin Kaepernick, the ex-NFL San Francisco 49ers quarterback who took a knee to the American national anthem, their spokesperson.

Nike's modern-day "heresy" equivalent of the United Colors of Benetton was met with staunch opposition and threats of boycott. Sales went up. To be sure, there are always going to be extremes, and even splintering of opinion within a specific position. For every We Company, there is a Chick-Fil-A. I mean, they trade in "straight" chickens! Regardless, this is their point of view. You may not understand it. You may not even agree with it. But surely, you'll respect it...or, at a minimum, acknowledge that it exists.

This is what it is to be a corporate citizen.

In September 2014, CVS Health became the first national retail pharmacy chain to stop selling tobacco products in their stores. CVS did this "because it conflicted with our purpose of helping people on their path to better health."

When Don Draper had his midlife crisis and his come-to-Jesus moment in AMC's hit show *Mad Men,* he took a stand. When CVS did something similar by turning its back on a "sure thing" like addiction, I'll bet many looked at them as if they were booking a one-way ticket to the funny farm.

They would have been wrong. Foolish, possibly. Brave, certainly. But not mad.

This wasn't CVS's *purpose* (that's just P.R. speak). This was a universal pledge on a shared mission, together with responsible and concerned citizens of this small planet. It was a concerted effort to suck less (literally in reference to those cancer sticks), and, at the same time, a resilient and compelling corporate commitment to survival.

When purpose meets action meets activism, you have corporate citizenship.

> ## "When purpose meets action meets activism, you have corporate citizenship."

The founder and chairman of the first company I worked for (Nando's Chickenland) had a saying: "Have fun, make money." I'd like to amend that statement to read, "Have fun, do good, make money." I'm pretty sure he'd approve of that change; in fact, I know he would. Today, he spends the majority of his time fighting malaria in Africa. Bill and Melinda Gates have become forces for change and good. Philanthropy at scale is a full-time job, and is often led by individuals in a post-corporate, semi-retired use case. I'd like to see corporates step up to lead this, and I'd like to reinforce the point that doing good and making money are not mutually exclusive. In fact, I believe....strike that, I *know* that it is unmistakably good business sense to be a corporate citizen.

In a commoditized world of companies that are built to suck, consumers will choose to transact with brands that exhibit leadership, spine, spunk, and attitude, and ultimately share a set of commonly-held values associated with acting responsibly, kindly, and positively to make this world a better place. It's just that simple, and hopefully, it's clear enough.

P&G Chief Marketing Officer Marc Pritchard echoes this by saying, "Marketing should be a force for good and a force for growth." The key here is the word "and." This is not an "either/or." As referenced earlier, it remains to be seen to what degree P&G walks their talk—and, more importantly, to what extent their customers recognize and reward them for their efforts.

Sorting the signal from the noise or "breaking through the clutter" does not apply solely to advertising anymore, but rather to every single aspect of a business that could influence a prospective customer, partner, or talent to align themselves with a company.

SECTION 4:

PRAGMATISM

CHAPTER 13

SURVIVAL PLANNING

W E'RE ALL IN THE SURVIVAL BUSINESS NOWADAYS, WHETHER WE
like it or not and whether we admit or not. The startup lives this reality
every single moment of every single day. Here today, gone tomorrow.
Secure funding today and live to fight another day; lose out tomorrow
and abruptly shutter the whole damn thing. Corporations know they need to
adopt a similar mindset, and are desperate to emulate their high-growth counterparts, or at least fool themselves into believing they can return to a state of
always-in-beta.

Here's a place to begin: consider yourselves permanently on DeathWatch. Be
perpetually paranoid, constantly self-aware, and recognize that the moment
you feel a sense of comfort and tranquility, that is the exact moment when
the water hastily recedes from the coastline, exposing the ocean floor, reefs,
and fish.

You know what is coming next...

DON'T WAIT UNTIL IT'S TOO LATE, BECAUSE YOU'LL
PROBABLY RUN OUT OF TIME

That isn't a Yogi Berra-ism, but a Jaffeism that really speaks to an organization's Achilles heel: their inability to move quickly. To make this a lot more
tangible, I'll give you a definitive time frame that could literally be the difference between life and death. Even better, it is empirical.

Between the years of 2004 and 2016, Boston Consulting Group's Henderson Institute analyzed the financial and nonfinancial data of all U.S. public companies with a $10 billion or more market cap.

They identified over 300 companies that had registered declines of 10 percent or more in total shareholder return over two+ years, relative to their respective industry averages.

What they found was that only 25 percent of these companies were able to outperform their industry in the period immediately following this decline. This reversal of fortune does not necessarily imply a happy ending—but it was a start. More importantly, spare a thought for the remaining 75 percent, who clearly needed to read the chapter on estate and succession planning (a different book) versus this one on survival planning.

But wait...there's more. If you call, click, or download in the next 30 minutes, we'll also throw in an even more radical finding: companies with a TSR decline over 2+ years of 20 percent or more were even worse off than the prior category's *Dead Man Walking*. They were in fact, D.O.A. Less than 5 percent of these companies were able to return to their prior performance. The remaining 95 percent+ either got worse or got stuck at these new, lower levels.

The implication is pretty unambiguous: if you can't spot the cracks in the armor early enough AND cannot take decisive steps to turn things around immediately, it's the beginning of the end.

The study also identified five success factors or variables that helped lead transformation turnarounds. They were (I have peppered in my commentary where appropriate):

1. **Managing investor/shareholder expectations (versus cost-cutting).** The CVS example is perfect here. Another example was when restaurateur Danny Meyer abolished tipping across all his brands in an effort to normalize compensation, from entry-level cooks to front-line waitstaff.

2. **A new vision and return to growth, with a specific focus on new business approaches or models.** This is my earlier reference to organic or earned vs. acquired or fake growth.

3. **Investment in longer-term strategic R&D initiatives.**

4. **Change in leadership.** The classic debate between internal vs. external hires.

5. **Formalized transformation programs, with a particular skew toward those that are larger (sufficiency) and longer-term (endurance).**

As a rule of thumb, always think AND versus OR. Companies that employed all of the success factors (grouped as long-term orientation, R&D, CEO change, and formalized transformation program) outperformed the next group by almost 2:1 with average long-run change in TSR outperformance of 17.4 percentage points. Easier said than done: only 4 percent of the motley crew actually managed to do all four, which is unfortunate, but not surprising. On the other end of the spectrum, 22 percent of firms hit only one of the four success factors, and for their troubles, they declined an additional 0.3 percentage points.

CHANGE THE BUSINESS YOU'RE IN

I believe that if you described yourself in just 10 years' time the exact same way you would TODAY, you're as good as dead. In some cases, companies have already drawn that proverbial line in the sand. Toyota, for example, is now positioning itself as being in the **mobility business** versus the automotive one. Nike describes itself as a service company. Tesla is a software company. This mass migration isn't around the corner; it's happening now! I wonder if you have a migration and/or transition plan in place?

Remember this from earlier in the book? *Uber, the world's largest taxi company, owns no vehicles. Facebook, the world's most popular media owner, creates no content. Alibaba, the most valuable retailer, has no inventory. And Airbnb, the world's largest accommodation provider, owns no real estate.*

Uber was founded in 2009.

Alibaba was founded in 1999.

AirBnB was founded in 2008.

Facebook was founded in 2004.

Average them out, and you're looking at a combined birth year of 2005. Fast forward to 2019 (when this book was published), and we have a period of time of just under 15 years in which the transportation, commerce, accommodation, and media landscapes shifted dramatically and irreversibly from predominantly durable and tangible asset-based businesses to those trading on distributed and decentralized intangibles.

If this book had been written 15 years ago, we would have been looking at the tween years of digital. Social as we know it would have been in diapers, and the smartphone and app nation in an embryonic state. If I had made the same statement, who would have heeded the warning, and who would have laughed it off as insane zealotry? I suspect some of the tombstones on the cover of this book might give you a hint!

The reality is that if I *had* made the statement, would I have said 10 years' time? Probably not. I would most likely have gone with a conservative CYA benchmark (that's Cover Your Ass) of 15 or even 20 years.

When it comes to predictions about technology, we are almost always too conservative about how quickly things change...or, should I say, unravel. As Billy G. (the philanthropic computer nerd; not the evangelist) likes to say, *"We always overestimate the change that will occur in the next two years, and underestimate the change that will occur in the next ten."*

I think it's safe to say we don't have the luxury of 20 years any more. Halving this forecast to 10 years feels right. Realistic. Prudent. Responsible.

Chances are strong that this will prove to have been too conservative.

Oh, well, time to get to the drawing board!

THE SURVIVAL PLANNING CANVAS

I created the Survival Planning Canvas because let's face it—everyone needs a canvas nowadays.

The first business-model canvas was created by Alexander Osterwalder in 2008 as part of the lean and agile movement, and it has inspired people like myself to create and distribute derivations under the Creative Commons license. I didn't use their tool myself, but you should feel free to visit https://strategyzer.com/canvas/business-model-canvas and to quote Simon Cowell, Randy Jackson, and Paula Abdul: "Make it your own."

If you like, you can scribble on the one in this book, but instead of defacing it, I would encourage you to visit www.builttosuck.com and look under bonus content, where you can download and print out as many copies as you heart desires. I would recommend enlarging it as much as possible and using a combination of markers and Post-its, filling it out in some kind of planning session or workshop with a "coalition of the willing" working group.

The idea behind the canvas is to get everything you need visualized and summarized on one piece of paper.

AHOY, THERE, ME HEARTIES, WHY THE NAUTICAL REFERENCES?

In 2018, I co-founded my third company, the HMS Beagle, together with the former CEO of J. Walter Thompson, Lynn Power. (In keeping with *Built to Suck,* JWT was the oldest surviving traditional or creative agency; however, they are now known as Wunderman Thompson, and you can determine if this is healthy evolution or the end of an era...). Our vision was to help our clients navigate the journey to survival. Two hundred years ago, the HMS Beagle set sail on its second voyage; it carried a certain Charles Darwin, who formulated many of his theories of evolution onboard. Paying homage to Mr. Darwin, we created a new planning discipline called (drum roll) Survival Planning in order to help companies plug the leaks and thereby ensure that their vessels were seaworthy (capability-building), fully equipped (talent design), and ultimately well endowed to set sail for the promised land (business transformation).

The nautical theme is rich in metaphorical analogies, and I hope you don't get seasick in the process.

THE KEY TO THE MAP

The Survival Canvas focuses on the third stage of the survival continuum: setting sail. It's designed to help you on a journey that may very well end up changing the business you're in. And if that sounds too radical for you, there are several other "wins" that may emerge, including—but not limited to—the ability to incorporate or adopt a new business model or integrate a new revenue stream into your existing suite of offerings: the "AND" approach.

The canvas is really designed in two halves: the top half is focused on discovery (guns backward), while the lower half focuses on exploration (guns forward).

Think of *above the fold* as a situation audit or synopsis detailing the present state of the nation, together with answers to the familiar questions: "Where have we come from?" and "Where are we going?"

Below the fold is your activation map in terms of how to get "there." At the highest level, "there" represents the continuum from survival to *thrival*.

Put them all together, and you have a comprehensive playbook to benchmark and triangulate against: as guardrails, markers, or checkpoints to ensure you haven't lost your way, and are "out to sea!"

There are two versions of the canvas: one for the corporation, and one for the startup.

With a bit more annotated detail, here is a bit of color commentary on each section:

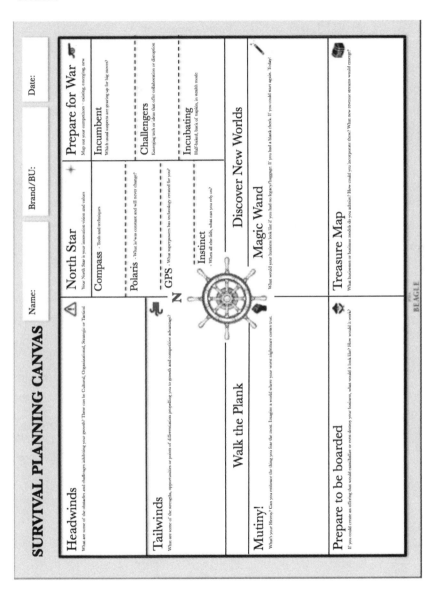

Figure 13.1 - The Survival Planning Canvas

Above the Fold: Discovery

Headwinds and Tailwinds. The closest comparison would be your conventional S.W.O.T. analysis. This is where you get to jot down and cluster the major forces (both internal and external) that are either holding you back or propelling you forward. I would challenge you to think a little more "big-picture" in order to get out of the weeds. Highlight major trends, obstacles, and points of differentiation that combine to reveal barriers to entry and exit for yourselves, your customers, and your competitors.

If the goal is to uncover opportunities in order to establish competitive advantage, focus on both current and emerging or anticipated forces. Consider which of these will be prioritized based upon importance and impact to the business. Which are most likely to be scalable and sustainable? Which are most susceptible to erosion and disruption? (Case in point: cell providers that held captive customers who could not leave them without changing their numbers—until they could....)

North Star. Your North Star is ultimately what will guide you on your journey. It is ever-constant, and even though you might not be sailing directly *toward* the North Star, it is your marker that will help you plot your path, stay the course, and, if necessary, course-correct. In consulting-speak, this section is designed to help you rediscover, reconnect with, and prioritize your core values. A cultural commitment to change is an absolute necessity, and without a firm handle on a set of innate beliefs, guiding principles, and essential values, you will be lost at sea.

Four fragments contribute to your North Star. They correspond (loosely) to the following:

Compass (and sextant). In other words, your toolbox, systems, and processes, as well as your primary strengths that separate you from the rest of the competitive pack. This value is a common thread that connects your attitude and aptitude.

Polaris. Ever-constant and ever-present. This is a core value that has been there from the beginning, and will be there long after you leave this earth. Where some values evolve over time, this one will never deviate or change.

GPS. Times have changed. Innovation and technology have created new and improved ways of being able to get from A to B better, cheaper, and/or faster. This value is likely to be your most current or recent addition to the fold. Or perhaps an extreme makeover or update of an existing one.

Instinct. When all is fails, who and what do you turn to? When the GPS is on the fritz, you've dropped your compass overboard, or Polaris is obscured by storm clouds, you need to be able to fall back on your gut, intuition, and experience. This value symbolizes your courage and conviction. It's something intangible and unique that sets you apart from everyone else.

Prepare for War. In the battle for supremacy, to quote Connor MacLeod and his nemesis, the Kurgan, "There can be only one!" If only it were that simple. If you know the movie *The Highlander*, then you recognize there will be many severed heads on the path to victory. Hopefully, one of them won't be yours! In this section, you'll segment your competitors into three categories:

Incumbent. These are the usual suspects, to be sure, but try to sort the wheat from the chaff. Prioritize the competitors that are in it for the long haul: the ones making big moves, especially on the startup collaboration and M&A front. Don't be afraid to step outside of your category (or comfort zone) to identify corporate pirates who could very easily invade your territory.

Challengers. Up-and-coming or emerging competitors may appear insignificant, but history (if this book has taught you anything) shows how quickly a competitor can rise and wipe out the competition. In this section, you'll want to list the high growth startups, both small and large, and highlight new business models or approaches from the marketplace.

Incubating. Who is the competitor that will put you out of business? Do they even exist yet? Like Ant Man and Wasp, you'll need to go subatomic to sketch out companies or concepts that don't exist yet. Remember the paranoid motto of the founder: "For every idea you're developing, there are at least five entrepreneurs further along the road doing the exact same thing...and arguably even better!" This section will feed nicely into the next ones, "Walking the Plank" and "Discovering New Worlds...."

Below the Fold: Action Plan

Walk the Plank gets into embracing your heresy, a.k.a. *mutiny!* And with that, looking to put yourself out of business or *prepare to be boarded.* Looking back to the competitive set, do you see an obvious category-killer emerging yet? Even if they are currently incubating or in utero, this is a classic opportunity to "just do it!" and start the thing yourself.

Mutiny. Are you ready to be a traitor and lead the revolt against the tyrannical status quo? Are you prepared to demonstrate the kind of leadership and guts required to define your legacy? List all the things you fear the most, or that represent the most extreme departure from what could be considered the norm. Now, can you embrace this fear? Meet it head on. Deal with instead of denying it. Run through the 10 heresies outlined in Chapter 7. Which apply to you? Perhaps you'll want to customize this, and create your own heresy endemic to your specific industry—or even your particular company and its practices.

Prepare to be Boarded. Once you have the bones of your heresy in place, put some flesh on them and build them out into a business concept. From an app to a service line, from vertical integration to line extension, there are many ways you can *pretotype* a concept and come up with an elevator pitch or premature business plan, or even secure some preliminary funding. Create the perfect cannibalistic product or offering that could potentially put you out of business, and then ask yourself two critical questions:

1. If the idea is so good, why aren't you doing this already?

2. More importantly, what are the odds an incumbent, challenger, or incubator isn't doing this already? In the case of the incubator category, your marching orders couldn't be clearer: if you can't beat 'em, buy 'em!

Discover new worlds. Putting yourself out of business is only half the fun. The real fun comes from putting everyone else out of business, and the best way to build your business is to start with a blank canvas. No baggage. No expected way of doing things. No bad habits. No politics.

Magic Wand. If you could do it all over again, how would you do it differently? Imagine and dream a future with no limits on ambition, imagination, or the ability to achieve any bold, hairy, audacious goals! Imagine you run the show AND you have a blank check. How would you stray from the path you're currently on?

Sears blamed their final woes on the burdensome and onerous pension plans they were locked into. I'm pretty sure had this not been a factor, they would have found another scapegoat to point a finger at. The digital-only banking sector[1] is growing fairly rapidly. Sure, many of them will not make it, but some will. From an incumbent perspective, it's almost unfair how easy it is for startups to enter an established marketplace, bending or even breaking the existing rules. In some cases, the market catches up. Case in point: Europe leading the way to levy taxes on the Big 5.

Your goal here is just to get on with it, and instead of complaining, figure out a way to play by the same rules in Honor Amongst Thieves (two can play that game!)

Treasure Map. Now consider how you're going to get there. This is part of your go-to market plan, and incorporates newer, cutting-edge business models and associated revenue streams, such as subscription or direct-to-consumer (often, these two are intertwined.)

THE SUBSCRIPTION ECONOMY

I've been stewing on this trend for a while, and I think it's opportune to take a few moments to highlight this massive shift, which will have a material impact on your business in the near future, if not right now. It's also the name of a book by Tien Tzuo entitled *Subscribed: Why the Subscription Model Will Be Your Company's Future—and What to Do About It*.

The subscription economy is all about moving from one-off, disjointed, or disconnected transactions to a continuous flow of revenue (recurring revenue). It's not like the idea is a new one (remember *Reader's Digest?*) What is new, however, is how this has exploded across the digital ecosystem and expanded into so many more industries, both new and old.

I can't think of a single industry that isn't prime for subscription. How long before we see the airlines getting on board, offering an "all you can eat" section of seats to a subscriber-only pool who can tap into this limited availability on a first-come, first-serve basis? You heard it here first, folks!

I recently purchased a new HP Printer for $20. Yes, $20. That's not even close to the remarkable part of the story. It's their Instant Ink subscription program that impressed me.

Figure 13.2 - HP Instant Ink

We went with the $3.99 per month "occasional" plan which gives us 50 pages of printing (with $1.25 per additional 10 pages), rollovers, and, of course, a continuous flow of ink cartridge refills. This is the Internet of Things in full survival mode! For what it's worth, it won't be long before the actual hardware is offered for free.

Tzuo (no relation to Sun) distills it to the following three attributes: data, relationships, and an experience (in this case, a subscription experience). He cites Apple's upgrade program as a great example of a subscription program that is more focused on building Apple IDs as opposed to pawning hardware (iPhones with a limited shelf life).

I recently purchased an electric toothbrush from quip, and I absolutely loved every aspect of the journey, from ordering to receiving my packages. Like Dollar Shave, it's a no-frills approach that strips out the unnecessary fat from the supply chain in favor of a great product and accessory set. Now, instead of freaking out when my $200 Oral B toothbrush goes on the fritz (again) or overpaying for new bristles, I have a constantly refreshed supply.

The graph below, created by Zeitguide and Ceros, reflects the meteoric rise of the subscription economy. Highlights include:

1. Amazon Prime and Spotify will have hit 100 million paid U.S. subscribers by the time you read this book.

2. Netflix now has 139 million subscribers worldwide (58.5 million of which are U.S. subscribers.) With 45 million Netflix accounts watching the film Bird Box during its first week of release and 80 million households within the first 4 weeks, is it any wonder that Netflix regards online game Fortnite as more of a competitor than HBO?

3. All hail Howard Stern, King of all Media, who has singlehandedly turned SirusXM into a phoenix reborn from the ashes of radio, with over 32 million fans tuning in to hear Howard, Gary, Fred, Robin, Sal, Richard, Ronnie, and sometimes even Benjy.

4. There is even a subscription service called MeUndies, which I assume is new underwear only. Proof positive that *any* business can thrive under the subscription umbrella.

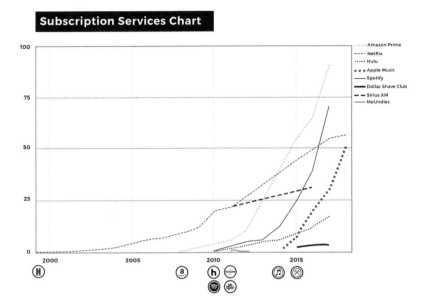

Figure 13.3 - The Rise of the Subscription Economy

As always, there is a cautionary tone, as well. Like all gifts with limitless potential, our default is typically to butcher the goose that laid the golden egg. Subscription revenue should not be looked at as easy money. The onus should be on us to raise the bar and hold ourselves to a higher standard on automatic renewals that are both explicit and transparent, or make it easy to unsubscribe or cancel.

Opting into a subscription (especially an intangible one, like an app or mobile service) is almost too easy, and typically comes at a pretty low cost; but over time, all of these micropayments add up, and can become cumbersome and exorbitant for consumers. Embracing your heresy with a customer obsession lens will go a long way toward earning and keeping the trust of consumer by building in a customer bill of rights that triggers inactivity with an automatic "freeze" cancelation notification, or even a refund for unused services, for example.

A WORD ON DIRECT-TO-CONSUMER

It's not just newer companies that make the list. Some people would include larger brands like Apple, Uber, Airbnb, or even Donald Trump—the world's first direct-to-consumer president—on the list. I'm less concerned about which companies make the list. Instead, I think it's better to focus on what makes them tick. Terry Kawaja, Founder and CEO of Luma Partners, outlines the seven characteristics of highly successful DTC brands:

1. Digital native/mobile-centric

2. Focus on product design/UX

3. Disintermediation (agencies, retailers)

4. Identity-focused customer relationship

5. Performance-oriented media spend

6. Content marketing for brand storytelling

7. Growth-focused marketing talent

How well do you think large corporations stack up against these seven criteria? Would you be surprised if I told you, "not that well?"

THERE ARE MORE MODELS...

There are other models you can explore; for example, one I call *Templerunomics*. In *Life*, after the 30-second spot, I said, "The consumer will pay with their time or their money for value." Fast-forward to companies like King or Supercell that have amassed valuations in the billions, largely from an elegantly-executed micropayment approach applied to a *freemium* model. Watching a video or paying $1.99 for a bundle of gems helps the new media moguls monetize their offerings. It is not inconceivable that console games will be given away for free, with 100 percent of the monetization coming from *Templerunomics*. If you think about it, that's a perfect heresy come true!

THE STARTUP VERSION

While the Survival Planning Canvas can be used for any business, regardless of size or age, there are two sections that seem a little out of place when focusing exclusively on new ventures: Prepare to be Boarded and Magic Wand. The former talks about putting yourself out of business, whereas the latter talks about starting fresh, with a blank slate. Startups are kind of already doing this—looking to put the corporation out of business by starting with a clean slate.

With that said, there is a fine line between humility and hubris. So if you're a startup and feel you want to take off the training wheels, as it were, and use the same canvas as your corporate counterparts, I say, "go for it!" It won't take you long to find a healthy number of holes in your reality distortion field, and if you don't plug them fast, one of your competitors (incumbent, challenger, or incubating) will.

Want an easy example of holding yourself accountable to the same standards exhibited by the big boys? What about offering REAL customer service through which frustrated or confused consumers can actually reach a human being? Have you ever tried to contact Uber customer service? Good luck, mate!

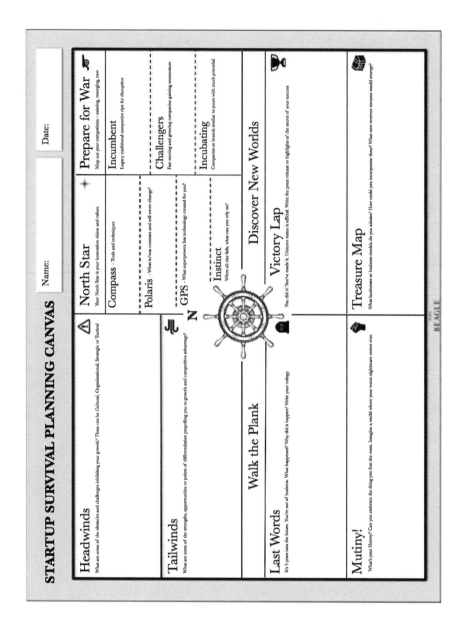

Figure 13.4 - Startup Survival Planning Canvas

And so for a company in its formative stages, gearing up for growth, or already on the hockey-stick curve, Prepare to be Boarded and Magic Wand are replaced with Last Words and Victory Lap.

Last Words. Write your eulogy or tombstone inscription. What went wrong? Why did you fail? How come you never got the additional funding you needed? Many startups avoid the inconvenient truth about their business, which is often more a function of human error than a nuance of the product itself.

Victory Lap. You've crossed the finish line in first place. Now you get to pen your press release or your award acceptance speech, bask in the light of your glory, and, while you're at it, get clear about what you did so wonderfully right! Also ask yourself if you're doing everything you possibly can to maximize this lever of potential.

As you did with the Survival Planning Canvas, you can download the startup version on www.builttosuck.com under bonus content.

BRINGING YOUR CANVAS TO LIFE

For both corporations and startups, your canvas is actually a map that will guide you on your journey to survival. On one piece of paper, you should now have a succinct visual overview of your current landscape, and more importantly, insight into where the puck is heading: a technological, competitive, and visionary triage. You should also have an idea of what the future might look like without the corporate shackles of a company that is built to suck, but instead with the freedom of a company that is built to soar.

If the key to success is to suck less, then the survival canvas turns this into a prescriptive solution as well as the formative stages of an action plan. Perhaps you've outlined an entirely new service line, or the wireframe of an app; perhaps you've resisted the tyranny of line extension in favor of a business-model revision or revenue-stream extension. Perhaps you're ready to draw up a brief and distribute it to your army of *intrapreneurs* inside your walls, or tear down those walls and extend this challenge to the public arena, utilizing your customer zealots. Or perhaps the idea exists already, and you're looking to accelerate, invest in, or even acquire the solution.

I look at the Survival Planning Canvas as anything from a strategic codex to an insurance policy of sorts. Even if things are hunky-dory at the moment, there will come a time when they're not.

The Hershey Company immediately comes to mind. Innovative in its time, and the first company to package chocolate bars, Hershey's built an entire village with schools for its employees, constructed theme parks to deepen family bonds, and took a chance on ET when Mars didn't. And now they are one of many "snacking" companies looking to lead the charge to becoming a nutritional leader. If I hear one more time how a snack (junk food) packaged-goods company plans to become a nutrition company, I'm going to puke.

If you can anticipate these changes now and even prepare for them, how can you go wrong?

So, how do you ensure that your Survival Planning Canvas doesn't fall into the category of nothing more than a fun offsite experiment? The answer lies somewhere at the intersection of a Venn diagram of ownership, urgency, and pain.

To make this a little more tangible, I filled out a survival planning canvas for the quintessential American beer brand, Budweiser. Using publicly-available information[2] on both AB InBev and Budweiser sales (both U.S. and global), together with some pretty well-known macro trends like the rise of craft beers, I created what you see below: a hypothetical straw man of a survival plan, and, eventually, a growth plan.

You can see where the Breathalyzer immobilizer idea would fit in, so feel free to add a sticky to the canvas, should you choose to do so!

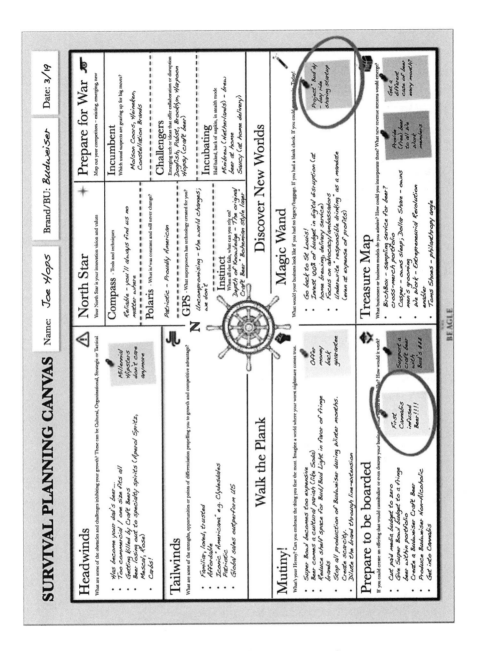

Figure 13.5 - Sample Survival Planning Canvas: Budweiser

DECONSTRUCTION OF AN IDEA

If the key outcome of the survival planning canvas is survival—and even thrival —then a key output is a plan that would incorporate fully tapping into the Entrepreneurial Revolution...which, naturally, is a lot easier if you already are a startup! From a corporate standpoint, the goal is to emulate the entity that is currently looking to put you out of business. By Walking the Plank, a company has three clear choices: build it, invest in it, or buy it. Based on the directive from the digital disruption chapter, route one is always going to be partnering with an existing company. You'd be surprised how open startups are to work with you. Just don't waste their time!

Of course, if you're a startup, the message is just to keep on keeping on, always staying a hair's breadth away from the prototypical pivot or course correction.

Whether you're discovering new worlds by embracing the art of the possible or getting there by slaughtering the cash cow, you'll want to wholly embrace digital disruption as a mandatory approach. In order to do so, I'd prescribe following the same curiosity-and-frustration path taken by most entrepreneurs and startup founders when coming up with startup concepts.

Most startup ideas with traction fall into these three categories:

1. Fixing something that was broken
2. Turning something from good to great
3. A fucking cool idea

FIXING SOMETHING THAT WAS BROKEN

Have you ever tried hailing a cab in New York City around 4 p.m.? Good luck with that. It's borderline impossible, as this is the time when the shift change occurs. Add inclement weather to that mix, and you are even further up the creek. The corollary is equally true (thank you very much, Murphy and your stupid law): when you DON'T need a cab, and they're swarming around you like angry, sadistic bees. And then two guys in San Francisco, who could never find a cab or a car when they needed one, started Uber.

And the rest, as they say...is history.

There's a lot of "stuff" that is broken. There are so many things we see, hear, witness, or experience on a daily basis that make us scratch our heads to the point of drawing blood in confusion, frustration, and utter disbelief. How on earth can this be the case? Why does no one say anything? Why do we just accept this? Why doesn't anyone do anything about it?

Exactly.

Or rather...why don't YOU do something about it?!

I tell founders to open their eyes and ears, and internalize their day-to-day pains and pleasures, curiosity and outrage in order to channel this toward an uncovering of the spectacular.

Try it for yourself. Write down a list of your frustrations (personal or professional) of things that are broken. The moment you utter the words *why doesn't someone fix this,* ask yourself why this can't be YOU (or your company!).

Here's one from my side. I can't stand politicians in general. They are dishonest, disingenuous, and infuriating when it comes to answering a simple question. They dodge, dip, dive, and duck it. More frustrating is the 24-hour, always-on news media that lets them get away with this, depending on which side of the fence they lean. They dance around the important questions, and when time runs out, they are pretty much where they started at the beginning: nowhere!

"Thanks again, Senator, for your time today."

"Thank YOU, Wolf."

Personally, I think news outlets should stand their ground and not allow the politicians off the hook until they answer the question.

Without an amplified outlet to the voting public, politicians would have an extremely muted platform or neutered pulpit, and, consequently, a tremendously difficult time maintaining top-of-mind awareness and relevance.

And so several years ago, I came up with the idea of creating a "Babel Fish" app of sorts. Using artificial intelligence, an augmented reality layer could sit on top of the talking head and provide an independent, objective, and accurate real-time fisking analysis of truth, truthiness, alternative facts, fibs, or downright lies. Think of it like a live fact-checking Twitter feed. It would get very ugly, very quickly. So what if there was a truth meter or horn that kept calling bullshit every time a politician tried to pull a fast one? We could even make it into a game with its own leaderboard—one you would not want to finish in first place!

Perhaps I should do something about it. There's still time. Perhaps you should, too!

FROM GOOD TO GREAT

Priceline is still one of my favorite companies out there. The simple idea of tapping into unused hotel rooms or unoccupied seats on planes to match against last-minute demand was sheer genius. Priceline took an already-working model and marketplace and made it better, using a bit of "gamification" and a simple database.

On the supply side, if the all-in cost of putting one bum in an airline seat was x, then x+$1 would represent a profit to the airline; and in the case of a last-minute travel scenario, even $1 would be more than they would have received otherwise. Of course, x+$1 also represents the absolute minimum amount (after fees) that an airline can receive....

Priceline was able to create an exchange that offered consumers deep discounts without adversely affecting the service provider's bottom line. In addition, it filled more seats (or rooms) ahead of time. This, in and of itself, contributed to reducing net supply and thus exerting upward pressure on pricing.

Before Priceline existed, people didn't exactly wring their hands in desperation, lamenting about the broken system of booking airline tickets or hotel rooms. Actually, it was quite pleasant with "analog" travel agents or online booking engines (aggregators and independent brands like Travelocity or Expedia.) After Priceline, however, consumers had even more choice and flexibility, while providers found themselves with even more customers and upsell opportunities, from extra bag fees to room service.

Perhaps you call it genius (the next category). I just call it simple economics and math. It also spawned an entire ecosystem delivering last-minute deals via dynamic pricing algorithms and crowd-based buying mechanisms like Groupon and Hotel Tonight.

A FUCKING COOL IDEA

I suppose you could say Airbnb (a website that allows people to rent out lodging) could fit into one of the first two categories, namely the "good to great" one. After all, the hotel-booking model isn't exactly broken. This might be true, but let's be honest; could anyone have conceived of the possibility that your mother would be renting out your room to a complete stranger? The same mother who taught you never to get in a car with a stranger (even me—you'll see what I mean later in the book!). Don't worry, because if they turn out to be a serial killer, they'll just get a bad review (assuming someone finds the body), and this will make it really difficult for them to get future victims...er, guests.

Airbnb changed the game by creating a completely new marketplace with more than just inventory from the existing pie. It created a new pie altogether.

This is the most exciting category of startups, because we are constantly seeing examples of people who are completely changing the paradigm of expectations, experience, and utility.

In many cases, the establishment pushes back any which way it can—explicitly or covertly—in order to stem the tide of change and disruption. This happened in July of 2018, when New York's City Council passed a bill that would regulate Airbnb host activity. Said a spokesperson for Airbnb: *"After taking hundreds of thousands of dollars in campaign contributions from the hotel industry, we're not surprised the city council refused to meet with their own constituents who rely on home sharing to pay the bills, and then voted to protect the profits of big hotels."*

Earlier in the book, I discussed a scenario in which, with the right brief and process in place, Run Pee could have been created for Myrbetriq (or one of their competitors)—unless it existed already, in which case it could potentially have been purchased outright! Using the Survival Planning Canvas, you can see not only how this scenario would have been "discovered," but also other potential solutions, including some pretty bold ones.

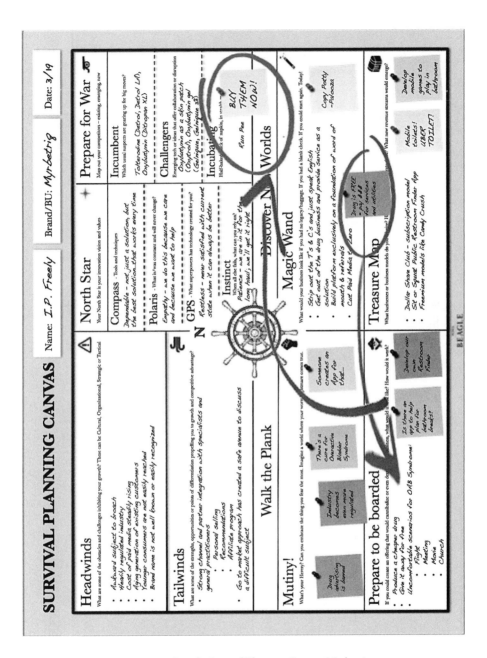

Figure 13.6 - Sample Survival Planning Canvas: Myrbetriq

LOVE THE JOURNEY

In *The Inevitable: Understanding the 12 Technological Forces That Will Shape Our Future*, the new book by founding editor of *Wired* magazine, Kevin Kelly, the author introduces the force of "becoming." *In the land of perpetual upgrades, everyone becomes a perpetual newbie.* Put differently, companies need to be in a constant state of metamorphosis, change, or evolution. Like a shark, they will die if they stop moving for even a second!

Along these lines, the journey to survival is a constant, never-ending flow. The only finish line is the cessation of business operations.

For this reason, the survival planning canvas is a constant work in progress, and, as such, it should be constantly updated; never viewed as an absolute, but rather a dynamic, iterative continuum.

A good starting point would be to put this on a quarterly timeline or time-frame.

CHAPTER 14

SELLING IN SURVIVAL

ARLIER IN THE BOOK, I MENTIONED SOME OF MY PET PEEVE QUES-tions I tend to get asked fairly regularly. In addition to *"what's the next big thing?"* and *"who's doing it right?"* another fan favorite is *"how do we sell this through to senior management?"*

I believe effective sell-through happens on four distinct levels; and in order for real, sustainable change to occur, it cannot happen in isolation. The four levels are as follows:

- Top-down: C-Suite Leadership

- Bottom-up: Millennials/Rockface

- Inside-out: Middle Management

- Outside-in: External Partners

Outside-in and **bottom-up** warrant the least explanation here, as they speak to entire chapters in the book, namely digital disruption and talent resurrection, respectively.

Collaboration with the external tech, venture, and entrepreneurial community opens up significant avenues and possibilities to strike up strategic alliances and partnership opportunities that can help lower the initial ante-up and perceived risk, and, ultimately, soften the financial blow.

The bottom-up approach highlights the younger and/or more junior work-force; the lean and agile; the optimistic, the untethered; the hungry and passionate. In other words, the bottom-up represents the uncompromised workers who are neither jaded nor politically corrupt. They're also the ones most capable of implementing the kind of radical change that, to them, is more *ho-hum* than *holy shit*. An energized base creates a company-wide halo that shines its light all the way into the boardroom.

Top-down: Speaking of which, change must invariably come from the top. If the buck stops with the top dog, then he or she must take the fall when blame needs to be apportioned. There are plenty of quotes I could share with you about what it is to be a true leader. Many of them focus on inclusivity, leading by example, empathy, and recognizing and rewarding team effort. That's all well and good, but in this case, real leadership requires arrogance, obstinacy, stubbornness, and the same qualities found in a real entrepreneur, including the ability to thrive inside a reality-distortion field. To get an entire company to venture out of their comfort zone, embrace their heresy, and embark upon an uncertain, unpredictable, and unstable journey requires immense courage.

Sounds great, but if it were that easy, everyone would be doing it.

There are more than enough corporate CEOs out there with Ivy League MBAs and all the right credentials. How many of them are able to make decisions that seem risky today, but ultimately prove to be genius? I read that the last movie ever rented at Blockbuster was *This Is the End*. It took place at 11 p.m. on November 9, 2013 in Hawaii. For those of you who recall, it was a movie about the apocalypse, and featured a fairly memorable scene with Jonah Hill and the devil (blush). Let's not forget that Blockbuster had a CEO (well, actually, several CEOs) who took turns playing the role of Jonah Hill in the afore-mentioned scene. And none was more infamous than John Antioco, who was at the helm in 2000 when Netflix CEO Reed Hastings offered to buy the entire company for $50 million.

It's important to single out attitude vs. aptitude when it comes to top-down leadership that is able to withstand the internal politics, dysfunction, and power struggles that ultimately resist and repress change. I'd also remind all companies that they fall into only two categories:

- companies that are in survival mode
- companies that are in survival mode

Take[1] ex-Governor of New Jersey Chris Christie and his decisive moves to reintegrate the UMDNJ (University of Medicine and Dentistry of New Jersey) back into New Jersey's Rutgers University. Back in the 1980s, the Rutgers Medical School had been taken away from the university for political reasons, and after many failed attempts by previous governors, it was Christie's efforts that eventually succeeded. Yes, there were some smart moves put into place, such as assigning a high-level assimilation team and "reaching across the aisle" to work to secure the necessary state budget, but perhaps the real key was Christie's larger-than-life personality. Christie's career was dogged by controversy, including the infamous BridgeGate, which occurred when several lanes of the George Washington Bridge were shut down, causing massive traffic jams. The act was an alleged retaliation against the democratic mayor of Fort Lee, New Jersey, for not endorsing Christie's gubernatorial re-election bid, and subsequently, it adversely affected his presidential bid. To be sure, he made some bad calls in his time, but he always trusted his gut, and there is precedent for suggesting that it makes a lot of sense to do so.

The University of Cambridge and Sussex published[2] a report in 2016 that concluded that people who trust their gut instinct are more likely to predict the correct outcome of events. Interestingly enough (and worth a read, but not immediately before or after eating), there is actually a physical science[3] that explains this:

Physiologists often use the term 'gut feeling' as a colloquial synonym for any intero-ceptive sensation that guides behavior. These sensations carry viscerosensory infor-mation and may originate from many tissues of the body, the heart and lungs, for instance, not just the gut....

The top-down approach must always draw on raw gut, as it is a positively primal instinct to survive. You'll recall that intuition is also a cornerstone of the value set underpinning the identification and positioning of your North Star.

So, if leading from the top and top leadership are so important, why isn't this enough to work on its own? Or even in conjunction with outside-in and bottom-up? More often than not, the C-Suite is disconnected and detached from the rest of the organization—without the cooperation of which mutiny is certain. The C-Suite needs to become the See-Suite, opening their eyes and embracing the reality of the shit show that is their corporation, rotting from the inside (and by inside, I am referring to the middle).

Of the four levels, **inside-out** is perhaps the least obvious component, but it is arguably the most critical in terms of potential impact—both positive and negative.

Inside-out refers to the plague—the festering disease that is middle manage-ment. They are the ones stuck in the middle, the ones most resistant to change and/or most threatened by it. They can't bide their time and wait out their days to retirement because it's too far away, so they dig in their heels and sabotage the whole kit and kaboodle. Welcome to purgatory.

Every company has this divide between the salt-and-pepper-haired C-Suite and the bright-eyed and bushytailed entry-level, and sadly, this bridge is booby-trapped with neurosis, paranoia, and a similar survival instinct that creates an insular corporate tumor.

The inside-out walking dead within a corporation are defined by both title and function. In my career as a marketer, I find this resides within the brand management category. Brand + Director = Pain in the Ass (not all of you, but most of you.) You might think the resistance would come from other *cosplayers,* like the advertising agencies. Not necessarily so. They're happy to be held accountable for their actions, if only the client organizations would open up their data treasure troves and share key business performance indicators and benchmarks with them. Also, the media or tech companies who would, likewise, welcome the opportunity to have a seat at the business table "upstream" as partners instead of vendors.

So, how to engage the support and buy-in of this mission-critical group?

Most people will point you in the direction of utilizing carrot or stick, corresponding to pleasure and pain. You'd be surprised how much people like pain. One alone can work, but together, they work even better.

THE TAI CHI OF CHANGE

I don't know much about martial arts or Eastern arts, but from what I have read, the principles of Tai Chi can be traced back to the Yuan Dynasty (A.D. 1271-1368) to a Taoist scholar by the name of Zhang San-Feng. It boils down to these basics: use calm against action, soft against hard, slow against fast, and use one technique to defeat many. Another way of looking at this is to use someone's undirected, raw strength and power against him or her.

> "When the opponent is hard and I am soft, it is called tsou [yielding]."

In other words, feed the negative energy associated with fear (of change, the unknown, being exposed, or losing one's job) with the positive energy of becoming a rock star—or making your boss look like a rock star.

That's the easy part. Feeding the political system you're trying to starve is literally on page one of Yoda's Jedi mind-trick handbook. But what if the problem is not your boss? What if it's you?

THE SUN TZU OF CHANGE

Jack Welch, former CEO of GE, said, "Control your own destiny, or someone else will." No doubt, his "former" company should have followed this advice, but I use it now as a counterbalance to the harmonious and peaceful Tai Chi process, and a sobering warning of what the alternative looks like if companies fail to take appropriate action. In other words, mutinous WAR!

In September 2018, the alternative investment firm Third Point, LLC, led by its activist investor Daniel Loeb, launched a proxy fight to replace the entire board at the 150-year-old company. Themed "Refresh the Recipe," the mutinous shot was sent across the bow by Loeb, who declared, "You're built to suck, and it's time to go...."

Figure 14.1 - Refresh Campbells

Third Point very graciously shared their presentation publicly,[2] and included in this deck was TSR data for Campbell's. With a 1YR TSR decline of 20 percent and a 3YR TSR decline of 22 percent, the implication was clear: *stick a fork in it, because you are cooked!* What do you think the odds are that Campbell's will be in the 5 percent exception of companies that buck the trend and prove everyone wrong? Don't hold your breath!

The proxy fight ended in November of 2018 with SoupNutsy agreeing to add two of Third Point's nominees to the board. Band-Aid solution to a gaping wound!

I HAVE SEEN THE ENEMY, AND THE ENEMY IS YOU[3]

Take a look in the mirror. What do you see? Are you repulsed by the reflection? Perhaps you should be. Or are you suffering from corporate delusional dysmorphia (C.D.D. for short)—the product of years and years of surrounding yourself with yes-men and women perpetuating a toxic culture of egocentrism and enablement?

Winston Churchill once defined **success as the ability to go from failure to failure without any loss of enthusiasm!**

So quit whining, and act like a winner. Why are you afraid to fail? Why are you incapable of being vulnerable and exposing your inadequacies? I assure you that your shortcomings are no different from any of your peers (inside or outside of your corporation).

Entrepreneurs are used to being told no, again and again and again. What if it's YOU who is telling them no again and again and again?! Why is that? I guess it's the path of least resistance. It's easy to get to no. It's so much harder to get to yes. Try it sometime. I dare you.

It's important to recognize your role in all of this. If you're not at the forefront of making change happen, you're part of the problem—implicitly, indirectly, or even passively. It's all part of the same gruel.

Let's be clear: **you can't expect someone to change their behavior if you don't change yours first.**

The corporation, as it exists, is broken. To build a company that will survive and thrive, we need to accurately represent the community we serve and the customers we wish to acquire.

This begins with embracing talent, diversity, and inclusivity across the entire organization, particularly in leadership.

With Indra Nooyi stepping down as CEO of PepsiCo, only 22 female CEOs were left running the Fortune 500 companies. Do I have to state the obvious? If there were more women running the show, perhaps this would be a shorter book!

The situation is so pathetic that in 2013, Martine Rothblatt was the highest-paid female CEO[4] in America, earning $38 million—and she was born a man!

Come on, people, let's jettison some of that testosterone in favor of some more estrogen!

The world is not waiting for you to catch up. Thirty percent of all DTC (direct-to-consumer) brands have female CEOs and founders.

And the problem isn't just with women. As of March 2018, just three Fortune 500 CEOs were Black. No, not 3 percent. THREE. That's the lowest since 2002.

MASOCHISTS RUSH IN WHERE SADISTS FEAR TO TREAD

Change happens when the pain of not changing is greater than the pain of changing. A version of this statement is attributed to motivational speaker Tony Robbins, and the gist of it is that pain is present either way, so ultimately, it becomes a tradeoff between the lesser of two evils.

Let's dial up the pain to a point at which the dominatrix in all of us utters the safe word *shishkabob!* (Hey, why not?)

Earlier in the book, I wrote about how true entrepreneurs are closet masochists. A true entrepreneur is not an evolution-denier or a blind believer in creativism— the divine power of the creative department to come up with a transformational big idea that will transform a business in 30 seconds.

Let's see if you measure up, and where you fall on the entrepreneur continuum. I want you to do a confessional...and be honest! With regard to your career/ corporation/startup, do you have pain right now? Can you describe it? How bad is it? How much does it hurt? Is it getting worse? And if so, how much more can you take? What is your tolerance level right now?

List it here if you like. Describe it in glorious, sordid detail:

_____

_____

_____

_____

_____

Now compare that pain to what it would take to make the necessary changes to deal with it, and hopefully minimize or eradicate it altogether. Is it really a fair comparison?

Actually, I'd rather hear from those of you who have no pain. Please email me at jaffe@getthejuice.com and tell me how great things are. How terrific business is. I especially want to hear from those of you who are doing business the same way today you were 20 years ago, and who foresee nothing changing over the next 10 years. I would love to understand how well you are future-proofed from the onslaught of technology, startup challengers, and the changing consumer taxonomy and business models.

Take me on. Let's go toe to toe. Push back, and make your case about why you are *not* in survival mode right now. Stand your ground. Take a stand. Argue your case—but you won't, will you? That's because you may fall into one of these four categories:

1. Those who think they know what they don't know (tyrant)

2. Those who don't know what they don't know (ignoramus)

3. Those who know what they don't know (bureaucrat)

4. Those who know what they know (coward)

The tyrant is, for sure, the most dangerous. They are control freaks: opinionated, stubborn narcissists who are deaf to any ideas that don't originate from their inner circle of cronies. Their extreme lack of humility makes any outside help repugnant. They are truly their own worst enemy. They slither and slime their way through an organization like a parasitic leech, and whether they jump ship or are pushed, they always seem to land on their feet. They are cockroaches, as Tobaccowala might suggest, and their toxic legacy is devastatingly permanent to an organization.

If you are a CEO reading this, you should demand from your leadership team a basic level of humility, honesty, and vulnerability when it comes to admitting weakness. You are not alone. Don't be like G.E.

"If the rate of change on the outside exceeds the rate of change;
on the inside, the end is near."

—Jack Welch

CHAPTER 15

SURVIVAL IS NOT A SPECTATOR SPORT

GETTING TO YES INVOLVES PUTTING YOURSELF OUT THERE. I'VE always believed that if you want to understand change, you have to be a part of it. You can't read about it in a book. ~~Except mine.~~ Even mine!

You have to "be the ball" and familiarize yourself with the change (that you most likely fear) firsthand.

Here's a personal anecdote, which I'm proud to share with you to reenact: when I became an Uber driver.

If you are in Fairfield County, I might just pick you up one of these days. I'll offer you water. Charge your phone. Offer you Sirius XM radio. I am at your service.

People asked me why I did it, and although the incremental revenue stream from the gig economy helped fuel my expensive hobby of buying gems in *Clash of Clans*, I did it because I wanted to understand and experience Uber from the other side—the inside.

As a parent, I wanted to get a sense of what my daughter's next driver had to complete in order to escort my most precious cargo. She's now driving herself, and I'm not sure which scenario scares me more. I'm kidding, Amber! Relax!

As a marketer and entrepreneur, I wanted to get a perspective of exactly how a valuation of $72 billion[1] could be created in nine years, and that just wasn't possible from the back seat of a vehicle.

And now, I'd like to share the initial findings of my startup ethnographic experiment.

APPLICATION PROCESS

Incredibly simple, smooth, and slick.

As one might expect, I had to upload my driver's license, registration, and insurance to provide proof that I actually owned a car, and also cross-check red flags like a suspended license, outstanding traffic fines, or a checkered driving record.

I used my Mac to apply, and didn't even need a scanner, as I just took photos of my documents with my iPhone and uploaded them directly.

Then there was explicit permission to conduct a background-check application, which was as simple as providing a social security number. What I liked about this part of the process was that I had the option to obtain a copy of my own background check, which I duly did.

You will be pleased to learn I passed with flying colors!

The final part of the process was to upload bank details in order to get paid, and download the partner app, which only became accessible once I had qualified and completed my application.

All in all, the entire process took about 10 days. That's it. I couldn't help but wonder how long it would have taken a Built to Suck corporation to (attempt to) do this. Just getting all the legal affairs and corporate communications people in the room to discuss the possibility would have taken longer!

MY FIRST RIDE

(You can't make this stuff up.)

My daughter was at the other end of town, and she was going to take Uber home. Before I continue, I should state that she was mortified to find out that I had become an Uber driver. She begged me never to pick up one of her friends in Westport. To be clear, this was less about any perception or stigma of being a "taxi" driver, and more about the fact that she was a teenager and her dad was a constant source of embarrassment in every department.

Unbeknownst to her, I decided to drive to her location and wait for her to request. Then I would accept her request and surprise her by picking her up. Now you can understand why she is constantly embarrassed of me.

I opened my Uber partner app, duly changed my status to "online," and began driving. A few seconds later, an incoming request popped up, and in both haste and shock, I swiped incorrectly and ended up accepting the ride.

IT WASN'T MY DAUGHTER!

I was now being diverted to a new location, and began navigating through the streets of Westport (at the required speed limit, of course) to pick up my fare.

What I didn't expect was the extreme anxiety I experienced at getting lost or being late, disappointing or irritating my passenger, and ultimately receiving a low rating from them. Thankfully, Waze came to my rescue, and the integration into the app where you can choose between Google Maps, Waze, or Uber navigation is pretty cool.

You just don't think about any of this as a passenger. You expect Uber to work. You don't think about the human on the other side of the screen, even though you know that the X in UberX represents ordinary people just like you or me, looking to make an honest extra buck or two.

Admit it—every time you see that car icon do a 180 and then another 180, or head down the wrong street, you get frustrated and annoyed. If Uber said three minutes when you requested, and it takes even one minute more because of, let's say, traffic (or a traffic light), that's JUST PLAIN UNACCEPTABLE.

So, as I'm driving, I'm wondering if my car is clean enough. I'm wondering if it's okay to have GPS audio directions read out loud via Bluetooth, or if that would anger my passenger, who might be on a phone call. I'm wondering if I should make small talk, or if I should have brought along mints, along with cold (instead of room temperature) bottled water.

If anything has come out of this, it has been a reminder to follow the words of Atticus Finch, and not judge a man until you've walked a mile in his moccasins...or maybe I should say, "Don't judge an Uber driver until you've driven a mile in his Honda Accord."

My first rider was a college kid home for the holidays, and he had just arrived at the Greens Farms train station. I was driving an Audi at the time, and I guess he didn't expect a German luxury car. A little intimidated, he sat in the front.

I invited him to try out the car's built-in massager. Nothing creepy about that.

I told him we were practically neighbors, and that I run past his house every day. Nothing creepy about that, either.

Perhaps I should have just turned myself in at the local police station?

He remarked how awesome my car was, and said he wished his first car could be an Audi. I was tempted to tell him that if he was diligent and drove for Uber like me, this too could be his....

We arrived at his parents' house, parted ways, and gave each other five-star ratings.

All was good in the world of Uber.

I was beyond relieved, and drove home triumphant with my hard-earned $7.

Ironically, when I told my daughter about it, she was actually disappointed I never made it to her. I think she just wanted her daddy to pick her up!

ENGAGING THE DRIVER COMMUNITY

Uber does a pretty awesome job at engaging its drivers. For example, in the first month or so, I got a text-message invitation from a community organizer to attend an Uber 101 class at a local Hampton Inn in Stamford, Connecticut.

There are also great tools for drivers, such as a community calendar of events that includes events like Lobsterfest on Saturday from 3-6 p.m. in Bridgeport.

It's also possible to see price-surging areas and drive right into them. Kind of like Storm Chasers. Or rather, Surge Chasers!

I also noticed advocacy and retention best practices introduced under the banner of "Partner Rewards." Drive 25 times and receive 20 percent off mobile phone plans.

Then there are gaming mechanics really designed to encourage drivers to stay "online" for as long as possible. Case in point: I was going to log off, but got a message to the effect of "Hey, you're eight minutes away from being online for one hour. Are you sure you want to go offline?" I guess I don't!

Along the lines of keeping drivers online for as long as possible, Uber has since introduced a feature that will only give you fares going in the direction you're heading versus taking you off course.

I drove another two times before "retiring," so if you liked the first story, you have **got** to hear the other two! I'll steer you online for two more laughs: www.builttosuck.com under bonus content.

This was my version of *Taxicab Confessions* meets *Comedians in Cars Getting Coffee*. Perhaps I should install a couple of GoPros and put out a web series! Moreover, this was my insider's perspective on the inner workings of a company that has truly revolutionized the world—and the very essence of markets.

DECONSTRUCTING MY LEARNINGS

A market is essentially broken out into two core components: transportation and payment. From the early days of bartering cattle or crops, the horse and cart were the key to facilitating a transaction. Today, we have Uber Cool, Uber Pet, Uber Eats, Uber Anything.

How long before Uber masters the payment side of the equation to complement the transportation and/or logistics side? How long before Uber starts its own bank? How long before the Visas and Mastercards of the world are left on the sidelines of the super highway of innovation?

Why has Uber succeeded? To answer that question, it's important to answer a question with another question: Why was Uber not invented or invested in by one of the credit-card companies, or a financial institution? I'll say what you're thinking: payment companies are not in the transportation or logistics business.

And that's *exactly* where you'd be wrong. They might not be today, but they may need to be tomorrow, if survival and evolution are to be ensured.

In 2004, when I wrote *Life After the 30-Second Spot*, I asked the question, "Will TV figure out online before online figures out TV?" I think we know how that turned out.

Here's another one for you. "Will Amazon figure out bricks 'n' mortar before Barnes & Noble figures out online?" Again, we know the result. Amazon's deal with the United States Postal Service to exclusively deliver on Sundays was beyond genius. It (arguably) singlehandedly granted a stay of execution for the postal service. Amazon's purchase of Whole Foods was quickly followed by the launch of their Amazon Go stores, where all you need to enter the store is to be an Amazon customer with a QR code from the Amazon Go app (yup, QR code). No scanning. No self-checkout counter. Just pick up what you need and seamlessly exit the store! You can see a video of my first visit to Amazon Go on www.builttosuck.com under bonus content.

Figure 15.1 - Amazon Go

And so, back to the question(s) at hand.

I would contend that it's just a matter of time before Uber becomes a bank, insurance, AND automotive company. We're already seeing this via their car-leasing partnership with Fair.com. Pick any of these established industries. They're all equally sucky, because they're all tripped up with the same dysfunction. And even if they're not, they have an egregious number of oppressive regulatory weights and obstacles to overcome. They're also part of an archaic ecosystem that does not obsess nearly enough about customers, as opposed to shareholders or business partners.

Did you know the credit-card business actually refers to banks as their customers, as opposed to the suckers maxing out on their debt and APR?

Uber does not conform to a category, or fit into a predictable container. If they are a shape, then they are the quintessential square peg refusing to fit into a round hole.

"The fax machine has gone the way of the dodo bird...and the iPhone will survive only if it keeps outperforming its competition. Typewriters and steam engines died in changing environments, but the Encyclopedia Britannica evolved, its cumbersome thirty-two volume set sprouting digital feet and, like the lungfish, expanding into uncharted territory, where it now thrives."

That quote does not come from a McKinsey article in *Change Management Monthly* or a Deloitte research paper. It's from Dan Brown's new book, *Origin*, which ironically describes the very essence of the computing process, and what is essentially a competitive advantage of a bot over a human. Now, can you imagine what happens when said bot is infused with (artificial) intelligence? Competitive + unfair advantage = pink slip, loser.

Truth is stranger than friction, no?

THE DAWN OF VERTICAL INTEGRATION

Perhaps you're not ready to change the business you're in completely. Or perhaps the transformation in question is just a little too ambitious.

So here's another approach. Don't change your business itself, but rather the *way* you do business across the entire supply chain or delivery process. It will surely lead to bigger and better outcomes.

Want an example? Actually, you've already come across plenty of them in this book. IBM. Apple. Nike. Amazon. Google.

The not-so-secret formula behind vertical integration takes us back to the artist formally known as Big Blue. Hardware + software + services/support + financing allowed IBM to play in several buckets at the same time. Today, the formula has a few different variations, including, but not limited to, payment (for example, subscription), which fits the financing component quite nicely.

Think about Amazon: hardware (Kindle) + software (Audible, App) + services/support (WhisperSync) + payment (Prime.)

Amazon Prime is brilliant. It is a common thread (subscription of course) that unifies the company's entire suite of services—past, present, AND future. It's actually an example of what I call *diagonal integration*, which is one better than vertical integration. Prime has allowed Amazon to move into businesses that it just should not have had any business being associated with. From original TV series or even movies like *Manchester by the Sea*, I still struggle to come to terms with Bezos, the bald-headed billionaire being associated with the Golden Globes, the Emmys, and even the Academy Awards. I'm beginning to wonder if the Oscar statue is actually Bezos!

When I talk about Amazon to audiences, I ask people for a show of hands indicating who is currently subscribed to Prime. Pretty much every hand goes up. I ask them to keep their hands up if they have no idea how much they are currently paying for Prime. Most hands are still raised. I ask them to keep their hands up if they don't care how much they're paying. You guessed it. A sea of hands still raised in the air...and apparently, like they just don't care.

Are you a subscriber? Do you know how much you are paying? Do you care? I'm going to try an exercise right now. I think I'm paying an annual fee of $79.99. Now I'm going to go and check.

Apparently, they increased the monthly fee in January of 2018 from $10.99 to $12.99 per month—an increase of 18 percent—but did not change the annual lump-sum fee, which remained the same at $99. So looks like I was off by $20, but if the annual price *had* increased, I would have been off by even more, AND I WOULDN'T HAVE CARED!

THAT, my friend, is what you call value.

Forget the tagline *what's in your wallet*. Instead, ask, *what's in my Prime?* The answer is, *more than enough!*

Here's another example you can try on for size. It's Nike: hardware (shoes) + software (Nike Plus) + services (Apple Watch integration, Nike ID) + payment (in this case, check out EasyKicks).

The concept behind EasyKicks is brilliant. It's a $20/month subscription service for a pair of Nikes for kids. When the kids outgrow their shoes (or even wreck them), they are exchanged for new ones. The recycled shoes are either donated to kids in need, or ground up and turned into playgrounds if they are not in good shape. In actuality, this example succinctly sums up the entire book—from embracing your heresy (in this case, Nike walking away from an established model of selling overpriced shoes that outlive their usefulness as soon as growing kids outgrow them) to a survival cocktail of digital disruption, customer obsession, and corporate citizenship.

It's also why Nike is a winner.

Finally, Apple: hardware (iPhones, iPads, iPods, AirPods, HomePods, Macbooks, etc.), software (iOS), services (iCloud, Genius Bar, AppleCare) and payment (subscription to AppleCare, Apple Music, iCloud, etc.).

Apple's i-cosystem is brilliant. They truly earn the bundled business, not by creating a walled garden (they used to be like this), but by creating an elegant, frictionless, and pleasurable customer experience—the likes of which we just haven't witnessed before.

I used to think Apple was arrogant to a fatal flaw in terms of what I perceived as a haughty, holier-than-thou approach to their customers. Perhaps this was influenced by their visionary leader, Steve Jobs. I was wrong.

Their customer obsession is sublime. They care so much about their customer and the customer experience...that they completely *ignore* them. They aren't running focus groups, launching surveys, or doing social listening to gauge the sentiment of the crowd. It's a risky strategy that only Apple can get away with, and it pays off with new product introductions like AirPods (30 million shipments estimated for 2018). And while their new iPhone sales took an unexpected dip in early 2019, it's best not to underestimate this company and their ability to bounce back quickly.

Henry Ford is alleged to have said, "*If I had asked people what they wanted, they would have said faster horses.*" Ironic, when you consider that more recently, Ford announced they would be ceasing production of all passenger vehicles except the Mustang! This approach has worked for Ford for the longest time... but for how much longer?

Amazon concurs, but does it all under the banner of customer obsession. To quote Jeff Bezos, "*Customers are always beautifully, wonderfully dissatisfied, even when they report being happy and business is great. Even when they don't yet know it, customers want something better, and your desire to delight customers will drive you to invent on their behalf. No customer ever asked Amazon to create the Prime membership program, but it sure turns out they wanted it.*" Bezos never detracts from a superior customer experience. He is always adding. Always.

For everyone else, the warning is clear: **professional innovators at work; don't try this at home!**

Vertical integration shows what is possible when a company becomes so embedded into their consumers' lives that increasing their presence across the full journey is a natural extension, and even an enhancement.

At its core, customer obsession anchors the journey to survival. As I mentioned earlier, it is the one mandatory pillar; but what about the other three? How do they fit into the plan?

The Henderson Institute on TSR decline and corporate turnarounds showed a disproportionate positive business impact based upon hitting more and more success factors.

I figure my four pillars should respond in a similar fashion, so do the math. Benchmark your current performance against the four pillars. Your share price won't lie. More importantly, if you can figure out how the pillars work together for your specific business, you can prioritize, optimize, and operationalize accordingly.

Directionally, this is what you NEED to take away from this:

1. If survival is to be ensured, a company cannot "flatline" on any of the four pillars at any time.

2. A company that delivers against all four pillars has an exponentially better chance of survival, but this is still not guaranteed.

3. Companies cannot scrape by when it comes to customer obsession. This has to be front-and-center in any survival plan.

4. Consistency over time is critical. Small changes over time can have a substantially positive or negative impact.

Nowhere is this more prevalent than with large behemoths except that in this case, I want you to look at this as motivation instead of a criticism. The Association of National Advertisers' CEO, Bob Liodice, calculated that just a one-percent change in growth within the U.S. corporate market translates into a $500 billion value creation delta over a three-year period.

Surely, one-percent growth is within the art of the possible?

STARBUCKS GETS IT

I'm in deep. I won't lie. I am practically gold for life, and so anything I say about the company is going to be tainted with bias. My daily guilty pleasure is a Quad Grande Americano with an inch and a half of steamed nonfat milk (topped off with a bit of foam on top.) I am a trainee's worst nightmare. My ticket ends up saying *ask me*. During the days when the baristas scribbled my name on the cup (nowadays, it's printed), I used to love it when they butchered it. Blame it on the accent. The first time they did it, they called me "Chug," and you can visit the hashtag #callmechug on Instagram for a few of the best ones.

Figure 15.2 - Call me Chug

I had a lot of fun with this, sometimes at Starbucks' expense, but I'd like to believe I was laughing with them versus at them.

Figure 15.3 - When Paul, George, John and Ringo went to Starbucks

I've always admired Starbucks based on their forward-thinking culture and inclusive approach to talent, like offering part-time baristas access to healthcare and stock options.

So I thought I would put them through the ringer and run through the four pillars to see how they would stack up (spoiler alert: they're going to score four out of four.)

1. **Digital Disruption.** With its mobile app, mobile ordering, Shake to Pay functionality, etc., there is a clear demonstration of leadership in customer-centric innovation.

2. **Winning the Talent War.** Earlier in 2018, Starbucks found itself in hot water when a local employee called the police on two "suspicious-looking" African Americans in their store. Turns out they were paying customers,

but this didn't stop them from being arrested! Outrage was widespread, and Starbucks' action was swift and prompt, with the closing of more than 8,000 stores in the United States for one day to conduct anti-bias/sensitivity training amongst 175,000 employees.

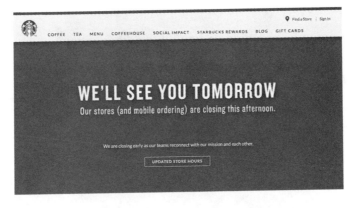

Figure 15.4 - We'll See you Tomorrow

Figure 15.5 - Sorry, We're Closed

3. Customer Obsession. With the exception of the two aforementioned African-American men, Starbucks wears its commitment[2] to its customers proudly, as a guarantee. If you don't like your drink, they'll make another for you.

Figure 15.6 - Our Promise to You

4. Corporate Citizenship. They recently launched an initiative called Mercato, in which surplus items are donated daily through a partnership with Feeding America to those in need. Another initiative, called Starbucks Service Fellows, allows store partners (notice they don't call them employees) to volunteer and provide community service through an external partner called Points of Light. Starbucks Corporate Citizenship is a global commitment that extends into 99 percent+ ethically-sourced coffee, a global network of farmer support centers, and pioneering green-building guidelines across its stores. It's not a one-off optic. It's part of the very fabric and identity of the company.

Figure 15.7 - Mercato

Starbucks describes their culture as:

1. Servant Leadership ("employees first")

2. Relationship-driven

3. Collaboration and communication

4. Openness

5. Inclusion and diversity

This is an active position that they walk, talk, live, and breathe every day. It's not creative copy concocted by an outside consultant specializing in "purpose."

I think it's safe to say that Starbucks has built a survival table with four solid pillars as legs.

Could the same be said for your company?

SECTION 5:

HANGOVER

CHAPTER 16

TOO LITTLE, TOO LATE?

You better, you better, you bet.

If you've taken anything away from this book, it should be the following:

1. This is not a drill.

2. See takeaway #1.

Seriously, you need to wipe out the phrases "test" or "test and learn" from your professional lexicon. Please stop the straddling. Stop "limping in" and doing the absolute minimum requirement necessary to put another check on your superficial checklist. By all means, if you're able to execute your "test" in next to no time and then seamlessly "scale with success," then you should go for it. However, if you're just going to procrastinate, spin your wheels and end up suffocating in analysis-paralysis, then I'm afraid the outlook for you is rather bleak.

You don't have time.

Take Office Depot, for example. In 2018, they issued a carpet-bombing barrage of press releases to tout their *Workonomy* initiative.

One of their employees anonymously posted one of their strategy slides to Reddit.

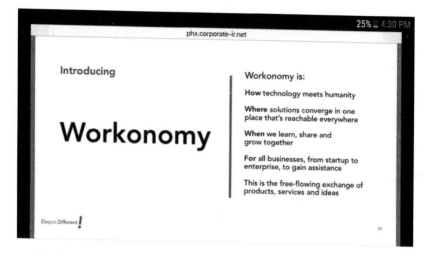

Figure 16.1 - Introducing Workonomy

Yup, this is how technology meets humanity. So, stripping out the corporate bullshit bingo, this is what workonomy actually is:

1. A hub pilot in Los Gatos

2. Tech services kiosks in 141 stores

3. Self-service print & copy kiosks in over 1,000 stores

4. Pack & ship capabilities online and in-store.

5. Investment in skilled team members and training programs from existing employees.

While 2-5 might seem like a poor alternative to FedEx Kinkos, the move to convert retail space into some kind of co-working or shared workspace is interesting....but surely too little, too late . Seriously, you're going to go head to head against WeWork or other "cool" grassroots initiatives? Pretty much the only way this could work is if it was given away for free.

Now, there's a heresy if I've ever seen one!

Unfortunately, the corporate geniuses at Office Depot didn't agree. Instead, they looked at this as a new source of revenue as opposed to a way to protect and preserve their core, fundamental business and business model: **get people into your stores at whatever cost to your company!**

So they decided to charge day rates of $40 for a "hot desk" for the day, a $400 monthly fee for a dedicated desk, or a private office for $750 a month, with a locked office door and "custom branding options." Can you imagine telling a prospective client you work from an Office Depot?!

And I'm not alone. Here are some responses from Office Depot employees, courtesy of Reddit:

Just flows right off the tongue. I guess the guy who invented Worklife is still working at corporate.

Stupidest fucking name. I knew it would be stupid, because the concept is stupid, but fuck, this is stupid.

Depot doesn't do any of this....

That's a lot of words that don't say anything. Surprised they didn't throw synergy into the word salad.

If I wasn't depressed, I wouldn't be working here, that's for damn sure lmao

In this unfortunate illustration, you can see what happens when a company misfires on the four pillars.

The world is not waiting for you to figure it out; nor will they miss you when you become worm food. According to the "Meaningful Brands" 2017 study from Havas, U.S. consumers "would not care" if 81 percent of all brands were wiped off the face of the earth. The worldwide equivalent was slightly lower at 74 percent. When consumer apathy and indifference affects three out of every four brands, it might be time to rethink everything.

The world is moving on. Take Brandless, for example: a company that manufactures and sells food, beauty and personal care products, and household supplies under its own Brandless label (the irony is awesome.)

Figure 16.2 - Brandless

It launched in July 2017, and already sells over 200 products, but unlike its "enemy," the corporation, it only has one choice for each food item, and charges the same price per item: $3. How? To quote Brandless, by *eliminating the brand-tax costs associated with marketing, advertising, distribution, and brand cachet.* Ouch!

I am not being a diva or alarmist when I stress that there may not be a happy ending in store for big business and their brands. To be honest, I'm not sure it's a bad thing if many (if not most) big businesses die out. Elizabeth Kolbert outlines a clear case, stating that we are in the midst of a modern, manmade Sixth Extinction. If it can happen to the third rock from the sun, it most certainly can happen to big business as we know it.

APOCALYPSE NOW

The cover design of this book reflects the *Corporapocalypse,* and no apocalyptic story is complete without its own version of the four horsemen.

When I started writing this book, I really just focused on a lone rider—**size**—as a direct link to inevitable death by suckage. Large companies, by virtue of their obtuse girth, had lost their ability to survive, because they have lost their competitive edge: their will and sheer determination to change and evolve.

As I talked to people about the book, I started getting questions like, "Well, what about Facebook? What about Google? What about Amazon? Are they exempt from sucking? Are they immune? Are they future-proof?" My response: "No one is exempt; no company will last forever. They, too, will go the way of Yahoo!, MySpace, Kodak, and the like...But not yet!"

And besides, Facebook already sucks.

I realized there was a second variable (or, in this case, horseman) present: **age**. I'm no ageist (I think I've made that clear), unless we're talking about inanimate objects, like corporations. Established legacy companies just can't keep up with the young bucks and upstarts. It's that simple.

My benchmark? Companies born after 1980 (Millennials and younger) are less likely (or more likely) to resist the inevitable urge: to suck. This condition, however, is temporary.

This was validated resoundingly by Jeff Bezos, who told his *employees* in November of 2018 that one day, Amazon, too, *will suck.* Don't take my word for it. Hear it from the mouth of Lex Luthor himself: *"Amazon is not too big to fail. In fact, I predict one day Amazon will fail. Amazon will go bankrupt. If you look at large companies, their lifespans tend to be 30-plus years, not a hundred-plus years."*

He continued by saying that their job was just to delay this inevitable outcome for as long as possible. Wow!

In keeping with the meta-four of an impending corporate apocalypse, size and age will represent two of the four horsemen. The third horseman—the kiss of death itself—is going **public**.

Becoming a public company is a natural progression of size. Or is it a side-effect? Like that four-hour erection after taking a certain blue pill? Sure, you'll have a prolonged good time, but it'll be short-lived, and you'll probably die. Once a company is a slave to external shareholders, you'll be praying for happier times when the devil you knew was the vulture capitalist. With the wolf of Wall Street at the door, your days are probably numbered as you saddle up, strap in, and get used to a vicious cycle of short-termitis in the form of quarterly earnings and the never-ending pursuit of acquiring revenue in order to maintain the façade of growth. Growth should always be organic. Not synthetic. Not purchased in a boardroom.

A public company is a founder's *Nightmare on Elm Street*, and its board represents a mob of cloned Freddie Kruegers (or at least that's how it appears to a visionary CEO, who stands before the board, guilty until presumed innocent.)

No one is safe. Not Steve (Jobs). Not Mark (Zuckerberg). Not even Elon. Perhaps that's why Musk had an alleged nervous breakdown as he essentially pleaded for the ability to take his company private again. For his efforts, he was fined $20 million and resigned as chairman of Tesla. Talk about an expensive tweet ($328K per character!)

 Elon Musk ✔
@elonmusk

Am considering taking Tesla private at $420. Funding secured.

9:48 AM - 7 Aug 2018

Figure 16.3 - Twitter Valuation of the Worst Kind

If the horseman of conquest is represented by size...

...and the horseman of famine is represented by age...

...and the horseman of war is represented by public...

...who or what is the fourth horseman—the horseman of death? At this stage, I'm not sure. Maybe that's a good thing for all of us.

Perhaps the fourth horseman is **YOU**. Perhaps you and people like you are the final nail in the coffin of the corporate reign.

Or perhaps the final horseman is **technology**—specifically, **artificial intelligence**. Musk seems to think so.

Or perhaps he has not yet revealed himself, which would be consistent with the one constant throughout this tumultuous roller-coaster ride: change.

Or perhaps the final horseman (and also the final straw that broke the corporate's back) is **culture**, or, more specifically, a lack of survival mentality or survival instinct within a corporation.

I have gone to great lengths and pains to make a case about why it is so important to create an environment able to embody so many principles that deliver against the "entrepreneurial revolution." In many cases, this might seem like something new for the corporation, but in actual fact, it's just a return to humble roots...to the beginning...to the garage.

Talent resurrection is just that. Awakening the entrepreneurial beast within implies that it was once fully conscious, but has since gone dormant.

In Jim Collins' book, *Built to Last*, he outlines 12 myths about visionary companies:

1. Great ideas are the foundation of great companies.

2. Great visionary leaders with charisma are the requirement of visionary companies.

3. Maximizing profit is the *raison d'être* of the most successful companies.

4. Correct core values are a common subset shared by visionary companies.

5. Change is the only constant.

6. Playing it safe is what blue-chip companies do.

7. Everyone finds a great working environment.

8. Great companies deploy brilliant strategic planning.

9. Fundamental change is stimulated from external hires.

10. The focus is primarily on beating competitors.

11. You can't have your cake and eat it, too (AND vs. OR).

12. For the most part, vision statements cause companies to become visionary.

Myths like change (5), risk-taking (6), and hiring from the outside (9) all speak to the mission-critical aspect and nature of culture.

So, who are the visionary companies cited in the bestseller? They include 3M, American Express, Boeing, Citi, Disney, Ford, GE, HP, IBM, J&J, Marriott, Merck, Motorola, Nordstrom, Altria, P&G, Sony, and Walmart. It's a pretty predictable group of some of the largest, most recognized companies in recent times. It's also a hit list of the next wave of companies that are, in fact, built to suck, with plenty of them showing visible signs of suckage!

On the surface, this might seem like a challenge to Collins' thesis. After all, we don't have to look too hard to single out companies that have fallen on tougher times of late. How do we reconcile this? Are they visionary companies, or not? Collins <u>clearly explains that visionary companies do not remain visionary companies forever.</u> Companies are not infallible, invulnerable, or immortal. Companies crumble when they fail to change, evolve, and adapt. As

Tobaccowala says, "Forget the phrase *the more things change, the more they stay the same.* Instead, consider *the more you want things to stay the same, the more you have to change.*"

Altria was once called Philip Morris, and it would appear that their 2018 call to arms to not rest until they had converted every cigarette smoker to their IQOS Cigarette Alternative is about as profound as their name change. It's a forced heresy, to be sure, and it doesn't help that the FDA dealt them a body blow in early 2018 by declaring that there wasn't *enough evidence that a handheld device that heats but doesn't burn tobacco reduces the risk of tobacco-related disease.*[3] Perhaps they could just bury those findings, like they did once upon a time. *Déjà vu* all over again! Not surprisingly, Altria invested $12.8 billion for a 35 percent stake in the e-cigarette Juul in December of 2018. A leopard doesn't change its spots.

Or what about our friends at G.E., and the sorry state of affairs post-Welch? G.E. was the worst performer in the Dow Jones Industrial Average in 2017. *The Wall Street Journal* ran a pretty scathing indictment of the state of affairs at Chairman Jeffrey Immelt's departure.

The new chairman, John Flannery, spoke about breaking up the 125-year-old company in order to focus on just three tracks: power, aviation, and healthcare. He wouldn't have stuck around long enough to see what transpired, as he was ousted in October 2018, less than one year after taking up the post.

Good luck, Larry Culp...or maybe you should change your last name to Gulp.

How the mighty have fallen—but perhaps it could have been different with a survival mindset in place. That's a tall order when humility and hunger are replaced with a so-called "culture of confidence" in the company, led by Immelt's "success theater:" a projection of optimism unmatched by the reality of actual business results, performance, and/or external markets. Immelt did not like hearing bad news—or delivering it. The result was a chorus of yes-men sycophants, enabling delusion, arrogance, and detachment.

IS THE ACCOLADE "VISIONARY COMPANY" THE KISS OF DEATH?

See what you did just now? You just jinxed us by calling us visionary companies. It's only downhill from here on in!

To me, Built to Last and Built to Suck are chronological bedfellows; sequential chapters in the rise and fall of just another civilization: the corporate era.

Maybe we should create term limits to being called a visionary company. Or maybe decline is just inevitable—part of the natural order of corporate life and the associated life cycle. Probably not worth being overly superstitious, as this is less about putting a target on the backs of companies (including Target), and more about conceding that size, age, being a public company, and culture are clear and present signs of imminent danger and looming disaster.

The answers don't lie in standardization, scale, repeatable processes, or order anymore, but rather in "regression:" thinking small, getting smaller, going back to basics and returning to a simpler time when the only rule that made any sense was getting to the next day, week, or month by getting back to day one. And the only way to do this was to surround oneself with like-minded renegades.

Companies built to last in today's operating times are chameleons: shapeshifters that are able to create systems to shock their systems into continuous evolution, and, ultimately, transformation.

GET BACK TO DAY 1

Everyone talks about Amazon as the gold standard today, in so many areas and on so many levels. You can't beat them, but you can try to copy them as best you can. Start with Jeff Bezos' concept of Day 1. What began in a 1997 letter to shareholders with "but this is Day 1 for the Internet, and, if we execute well, for Amazon.com" was continued 20 years later, in his 2017 letter to shareholders: *"Jeff, what does Day 2 look like?' That's a question I just got at our most recent all-hands meeting. I've been reminding people that it's Day 1 for a couple of decades. Day 2 is stasis. Followed by irrelevance. Followed by excruciating, painful decline. Followed by death. And that is why it is always Day 1."*

Do a Google search for Bezos' Day 1 philosophy, and you'll quickly find both of these letters. The cliff-notes version/highlights:

- **True Customer Obsession.** *I think someone wrote a book on that....*

- **Resist Proxies.** *When process becomes a proxy, it becomes superior to the actual results. So if you're not getting the results you expect, change the process!*

- **Look outside the company/embrace external trends.** *Score one for "digital disruption."*

- **High-Velocity Decision-Making.** *Make decisions quickly, even with limited information, and incorporate things like "disagree and commit."*

Living in a constant state of Day 1 is like living a constant state of beta, which is both exhilarating and exhausting!

Remember, the survival instinct is triggered by two powerful drivers: self-preservation (I don't want to die; I want to survive) and adaptation (I want to thrive.)

As hard as the road ahead might seem, it is a defined path, and you should take solace in that. You know what to do. Identifying and fast-tracking young and rising talent on one end. Leadership training on the other. And let's not forget the middle. Forget it at your peril.

I offer my strategic framework as a working hypothesis, supported by personal anecdotes, illustrative case studies, and good old common sense. I hope you will help me on this journey to transform the transition from anecdotal to empirical.

I invite you to visit www.builttosuck.com, where you will find a number of ways to continue the conversation with me. Feel free to contact me directly, as well, at jaffe@getthejuice.com or @jaffejuice on most hubs (including Venmo.....hint, hint).

FINAL WORDS

As I was about to submit my manuscript, I went back and looked at the very top of the Fortune 500 companies from 1955 and wondered, *where are they now?*

Take DuPont. Tenth on the list in 1955. 113th on the list in 2017. Founded in 1802 as a gunpowder mill. Today, the mission is about "solving global challenges—rooted in our science and engineering expertise." I'm assuming gunpowder is not a part of this solution, but I could be wrong.

As for the rest, you'll notice familiar recurring industries dominating the list then, but no longer today: steel and oil. Gas still lives large, but has since dramatically consolidated. And in a world of self-driving electric cars, how much longer will this persist?

As for the others, there is a general focus on things like meat, and durables like automotive, tires, and planes. "Things" that could be called commodities today.

I couldn't help but wonder how many of these companies saw the writing on the wall. If they did, could they have pivoted or transformed, and changed the businesses they were in?

Today, the Fortune 500 is dominated by companies in the technology, health-care, and retail space. I can spot two endangered species out of those three categories. Sell. Sell. Sell.

I leave you with these thoughts:

1. What is tomorrow's steel? Oil? Tobacco? Is it your industry? Is it your business?

2. When it's your time to expire, will you go quietly, gently, and peacefully into the night? After all, if death is inevitable, why not just embrace it?

3. Can you avoid looking back in regret in 10 years or less, saying, "If only we had done something about it!"

Like Sears.

The afterword of this book is an op-ed piece that was written by Gord Hotchkiss back in June of 2017. Sears filed for bankruptcy in October of 2018. I can't help but wonder what would have happened had Sears gotten hold of the Survival Planning Canvas back then. Even so, do you think they would have done anything about it?

Maybe you will be different.

Look to the examples of companies in this book that have bucked the trends and resisted the urge to suck. The sincerest form of flattery is imitation, so copy them. Emulate them. Learn from them.

Your journey ahead will be filled with contradictions. I think it's important to recognize that there is no definitive or absolute path that is a sure thing. The very nature of venturing into the unknown assumes unpredictable outcomes. You're encouraged to make the attempt and be prepared to fail, but this doesn't happen in a vacuum. Without the support of the entire organization, any momentum is often short-lived. The worst thing you could ever say or hear is *we tried that once*. Despite all of the uncertainty and unpredictability, my message to you is this: it's still worth it. Don't give up. Don't give in.

You have the ability. You have the power. You've seen the future. Now make sure there is a future! Fight for the future. Fight for survival.

The clock is ticking....

Joseph Jaffe will return in 2021.

THE DEATH OF SEARS, THE EDGE OF CHAOS

So, here's the question. Could Sears—the retail giant that has become the poster child for the death of mall-based retail shopping—have saved itself?

This is an important question, because I don't think Sears' downward trend is an isolated incident.

In 2006, historian Richard Longstreth explored the rise and fall of Sears. The rise is well-chronicled. From the store's beginnings in 1886, the team of Richard Sears and Alvah Roebuck grew to dominate the catalog mail-order landscape. They prospered by creating a new way of shopping that catered specifically to the rural market of America, a rapidly expanding opportunity created by the Homestead Act of 1862.

The spread of railroads across the continent through the 1860s and '70s allowed Sears to distribute physical goods across the nation. This, combined with their quality guarantee and free return policy, allowed the retailer to grow rapidly to a position of dominance.

In the 1920s and '30s, Robert E. Wood, the fourth president of Sears, took the company in a new direction. He reimagined the concept of a physical retail store, convincing the reluctant company to expand from its very lucrative catalog business.

This move was directly driven by Sears' foundation as a mail-order business. In essence, Wood was hedging his bet. He built his stores far from downtown business centers, where land was cheap. And, if they failed as retail destinations, they could always be repurposed as mail-order distribution and fulfillment centers.

But Wood got lucky. Just about the time he made this call, America fell in love with the automobile. They didn't mind driving a little bit to get to a store where they could save some money. This was followed by the suburbanization of America. When America moved to the suburbs, Sears was already there.

So, you could say Sears was amazingly smart with its strategy, presciently predicting two massive disruptions in the history of consumerism in America. Or you could also say that Sears got lucky and the market happened to reward it—twice. In the language of evolution, two fortuitous mutations of Sears led to it being naturally selected by the marketplace.

But, as Longstreth showed, the company's luck ran out on the third disruption: the move to online shopping.

A recent article looking back at Longstreth's paper is titled, "Could Sears Have Avoided Becoming Obsolete?"

I believe the answer is no. The article points to one critical strategic flaw as the reason for Sears' non-relevance: doubling down on its mall-anchor strategy as the world stopped going to malls. In hindsight, this seems correct, but the fact is, it was no longer in Sears' DNA to pivot into new retail opportunities. It couldn't have jumped on the ecommerce bandwagon, just as a whale can't learn how to fly.

It's easy for historians to cast a gaze backward and find reasons for organizational failure, just as it's easy to ascribe past business success to a brilliant strategy or a visionary CEO.

The fact is, as business academic Phil Rosenzweig shows in his masterful book *The Halo Effect*, we're just trying to jam history into a satisfying narrative. And narratives crave cause and effect. We look for mistakes that lead to obsolescence. This gives us the illusion that we could avoid the same fate if we're smarter.

It's not that simple, though. There are bigger forces at play here. And they can be found at the edge of chaos.

EDGE OF CHAOS THEORY

In his book *Complexity: Life at the Edge of Chaos*, Roger Lewin chronicles the growth of the Santa Fe Institute, an academic think tank dedicated to exploring complexity for the last 33 years.

The "big idea" in Lewin's book is the edge of chaos theory, a term coined by mathematician Doyne Farmer to describe a discovery by computer scientist Christopher Langton.

The theory, in its simplest form, is this: on one side, you have chaos, where there is just too much dynamic activity and instability for anything sustainable to emerge. On the other side, you have order, where rules and processes are locked in, and things become frozen solid. These are two very different states that can apply to biology, sociology, chemistry, physics, economics—pretty much any field you can think of.

To go from one state—in either direction—is a phase transition. Everything changes when you move from one to the other. On one side, turmoil crushes survivability. On the other, inertia smothers change.

In between is a razor-thin interface, balanced precipitously at the edge of chaos. Theorists believe that it's in this delicate interface that life forms, creativity happens, and new orders are born.

For any single player, it's almost impossible to maintain this delicate balance. As organizations grow, I think they naturally move from chaos to order, at some point moving through this exceptional interface where the magic happens.

Some companies manage to move through this space a few times. Apple is such a company. Sears probably moved through the space twice, once in the setup of its mail-order business and once in its move to suburban retail.

Sooner or later, organizations go through their typical life cycle, and inevitably choose order over chaos. At this point, their DNA solidifies to the point that they can no longer rediscover the delicate interface between the two.

We all love to believe that immortality can be captured in our corporate form, whether that be our company or our own body. But history shows that we all have a natural life cycle. We may be lucky enough to extend our duration in that interface on the edge of chaos, but sooner or later, our time there will end. Just as it did with Sears.

—Gord Hotchkiss, Out of my Gord Consulting

ENDNOTES

A note about the cover

1. My thanks to my panelists: Sebastian Grodzietzki, Howard Wiener, MSIA, PMP, Glenn Wastyn, Bill Donohoo, Alan Arnett, Jim Kelly, Patty Soltis MBA BS, Alan Arnett, Frank Mendoza, Greg Moran, Dave Saxby and Chris Woods

Preface

1. See: boiling frog syndrome

Chapter 1

1. Bob Liodice, ANA CEO, at his opening Masters of Marketing address in 2018

Chapter 2

1. The Tricorder X Grand Prize was awarded to Dr. Basil Harris, an emergency room physician, and his brother George Harris, a network engineer. The team beat more than 300 teams from 38 countries in an initiative underwritten by Qualcomm.

2. http://www.npr.org/sections/thetwo-way/2016/07/06/484988211/half-a-million-hoverboards-recalled-over-risk-of-fire-explosions

Chapter 3

1. There's an article suggesting that this isn't exactly true—goldfish don't have short attention spans, and human attention spans are not shrinking. I started reading it, but then got distracted by an incoming text message, and forgot all about it. (source: http://www.bbc.com/news/health-38896790).

Chapter 4

1. FastCompany, *Why Most Venture-Backed Companies Fail* (2017)

2. The Second Industrial Revolution, also known as the Technological Revolution, was a phase of the larger Industrial Revolution corresponding to the latter half of the 19th century until World War I. It is considered to have begun with Bessemer steel in the 1860s and culminated in mass production and the production line. (Wikipedia)

3. https://theweek.com/articles/731835/golden-age-startups-over

Chapter 6

1. https://people.com/food/mcdonalds-touchscreens-feces-bacteria-uk/

2. Wikipedia

3. https://io9.gizmodo.com/5886602/ten-amazing-and-occasionally-explosive-chemical-reactions-caught-on-video

Chapter 7

1. Author, *The Big Pivot* and *Green to Gold*; advisor/speaker on how companies navigate mega-challenges.

2. https://www.theguardian.com/technology/2018/aug/02/apple-becomes-worlds-first-trillion-dollar-company

3. https://www.marketwatch.com/story/nra-donors-respond-to-imminent-threat-but-long-term-finances-are-shaky-2018-03-29

Chapter 8

1. https://www.zdnet.com/article/ibm-shows-growth-after-22-straight-quarters-of-declining-revenues-but-has-it-turned-the-corner/

Chapter 9

1. Hat tip to Richard Eisert

2. https://www.entrepreneur.com/dbimages/article/where-startup-funding-really-comes-from-infographic.jpg

3. be talking Martian (this is the nickname for an unconventional representation of Chinese characters)

Chapter 10

1. Park Communications

2. Whitney Houston, The Greatest Love of All

3. https://exitround.com/acquihires-from-2005-to-today-from-hype-to-pragmatism/

Chapter 11

1. Missy Elliot, *Work It*

2. https://blog.kissmetrics.com/how-netflix-uses-analytics/

3. https://hbr.org/1993/01/customer-intimacy-and-other-value-disciplines

Chapter 12

1. I'm being sarcastic in case you can't see my face.

2. Alexander Hamilton

Chapter 14

1. https://thefinancialbrand.com/69560/25-direct-online-digital-banks/

2. https://money.cnn.com/2018/05/09/investing/anheuser-busch-in-bev-budweiser-beer-earnings/index.html

3. Excerpted from Jim Kelly's contribution on currnt

4. https://bigthink.com/articles/why-you-should-trust-your-gut-according-to-the-university-of-cambridge

5. https://www.nature.com/articles/srep32986

6. www.builttosuck.com/refreshcampbells

7. Walt Kelly's comic strip *Pogo,* 1971

8. CEO, United Therapeutics

Chapter 15

1. https://www.recode.net/2018/2/9/16996834/uber-latest-valuation-72-billion-waymo-lawsuit-settlement

2. https://customersrock.wordpress.com/2008/02/29/re-experiencing-starbucks-update-3-the-training/

Chapter 16

1. https://www.wsj.com/articles/iqos-cigarette-alternative-gets-mixed-reception-from-fda-panel-1516907799

INDEX